P9-CLN-831

Opera
Guide 31

Siegfried (Alberto Remedios) and Brünnhilde (Rita Hunter) in the Prelude of the ENO production by Glen Byam Shaw and John Blatchley, designed by Ralph Koltai; 1977 (photo: John Garner)

Preface

This series, published under the auspices of English National Opera and The Royal Opera, aims to prepare audiences to enjoy and evaluate opera performances. Each book is the product of many hands. The Guides to *The Ring of the Nibelung* contain Wagner's text and the translation by Andrew Porter, with a list of musical leitmotifs. The accompanying essays have been commissioned to give an insight into each work, as well as a perspective on the cycle as a whole.

Nicholas John
Series Editor

31

Twilight of the Gods
Götterdämmerung

Richard Wagner

Opera Guide Series Editor: Nicholas John

Published in association with
English National Opera and The Royal Opera

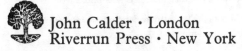

John Calder · London
Riverrun Press · New York

First published in Great Britain, 1985 by
John Calder (Publishers) Ltd.,
18 Brewer Street,
London W1R 4AS

First published in the U.S.A., 1985 by
Riverrun Press Inc.,
1170 Broadway,
New York, NY 10001

Copyright © English National Opera and The Royal Opera 1985
An Introduction to the End © Michael Tanner 1985
Motif, Memory and Meaning in 'Twilight of the Gods' © Robin Holloway 1985
The Questionable Lightness of Being: Brünnhilde's Peroration to 'The Ring' ©
Christopher Wintle 1985

The Ring of the Nibelung English translation © Andrew Porter, 1976
Printed by arrangement with Faber Music Ltd, London and W.W. Norton & Company
Inc., New York (U.S.A. rights). All rights, including *inter alia* the right of performance
with music and reproduction by any means or in any form, strictly reserved.

ALL RIGHTS RESERVED

BRITISH LIBRARY CATALOGUING IN PUBLICATION DATA
Wagner, Richard, *1813-1883*
  Twilight of the Gods.—(Opera guide; 31)
  1. Operas—Librettos
  I. Title   II. Porter, Andrew   III. Series
  782.1'2   ML50.W14

LIBRARY OF CONGRESS CATALOGING IN PUBLICATION DATA

Wagner, Richard, 1813-1883.
  [Ring des Nibelungen. Götterdämmerung. Libretto. English & German.]
  Twilight of the Gods.

  (Opera guide; 31)
  Includes libretto, with English translation by Andrew Porter, and commentary.
  Discography: p.
  Bibliography: p.
  1. Operas — Librettos.   2. Wagner, Richard, 1813-1883.
Ring des Nibelungen. Götterdämmerung.   I. Porter, Andrew, 1928-
II. Title.   III. Series.
ML50.W14R72 1985   782.1'092'4   85-790

ISBN 0-7145-4063-3

SUBSIDISED BY THE
Arts Council
OF GREAT BRITAIN

John Calder (Publishers) Ltd, English National Opera and
The Royal Opera House, Covent Garden Ltd receive
financial assistance from the Arts Council of Great Britain.
English National Opera also receives financial assistance from
the Greater London Council.

No part of this publication may be reproduced, stored in a retrieval system, or
transmitted, by any form or by any means, electronic, mechanical, photocopying or
otherwise, except brief extracts for the purpose of review, without the prior written
permission of the copyright owner and publisher.

Any paperback edition of this book whether published simultaneously with, or
subsequent to, the hardback edition is sold subject to the condition that it shall not, by
way of trade, be lent, resold, hired out, or otherwise disposed of, without the publisher's
consent, in any form of binding other than that in which it is published.

Typeset in Plantin by Margaret Spooner Typesetting, Dorchester, Dorset
Printed by the Camelot Press Ltd., Southampton

Contents

List of Illustrations

Picture research: Henrietta Bredin

An Introduction to the End

Michael Tanner

No-one who has thought at all about *The Ring* has failed to find the ending of the whole work problematic. Naturally the first person to do so was Richard Wagner, the most eloquent testimony to his unease being the number of different versions that he wrote for it. Commentators on the ending, notably Ernest Newman[1], Carl Dahlhaus[2], and John Deathridge[3], have traced the differences in great detail. Their investigations are extraordinarily fascinating and illuminating about Wagner's vacillations, even if one doesn't agree with Dahlhaus that 'to persevere rigorously in the postulate that one must understand a text entirely in itself, if one is trying to treat it as a work of art and not as a document, would in the case of *Götterdämmerung* mean a grievous sacrifice of understanding'[4], especially since he concludes that, 'the first conception of the work is at the same time the last'[5]. Following the genesis and development of Wagner's drafts of *The Ring*, both in prose and verse, is absorbing but in the last resort what we have to respond to and judge is what Wagner actually composed, and no amount of scholarship will enable us to solve problems that we find there, even if we are helped, as I think we certainly are, to see how they came about.

Grateful, therefore, for the research done by the scholars I've mentioned and others, I want to look only at the finished product and see whether it makes sense, and if so, what that sense is. Wagner himself never ceased to insist that one could only fully understand what *The Ring* meant when one responded to it as a total entity, that is to the music and the spectacle as well as the words. He made that clear in a letter to his former comrade in revolution, August Roeckel, when he wrote 'I feel that, at a good performance, the most simple-minded spectator will be in no doubt as to that point'[6], referring to Roeckel's question as to why, since the gold is returned to the Rhine, the gods still perish. Wagner continues: 'It has to be admitted that the downfall of the gods does not arise of necessity out of counterpoints. These can indeed be interpreted, turned and twisted in all kinds of ways ... No, the necessity of this downfall springs from our innermost feelings, as it does from the innermost feelings of Wotan. It was thus important to justify this necessity *by feeling*: and this happens of itself when the feeling follows the total action, with all its simple, natural motives, in complete sympathy from beginning to end. When finally Wotan gives expression to this necessity he only says what we ourselves already feel must needs be. When Loge, at the end of *The Rhinegold*, calls out after the gods, as they make their way towards Valhalla, "They hasten towards their end who deem their power to be so enduring", in that moment he only gives expression to our own thought, for anyone who has

1 Ernest Newman: *The Life of Richard Wagner*, Volume Two, pp. 347-361. (London, 1937).
2 Carl Dahlhaus: Uber den Schluss der *Götterdämmerung*, in *Richard Wagner: Werk und Wirkung* (Regensburg, 1971).
3 John Deathridge, in an article in *Nineteenth Century Music*, forthcoming.
4 Dahlhaus, *loc. cit.*, p. 97.
5 Dahlhaus, *loc. cit.*, p. 115.
6 quoted by Newman, *loc. cit.*, p. 359.

The final conflagration: an illustration from 'The Sphere', May 10, 1913 (Royal Opera House Archives)

followed this prelude [*Rhinegold*] sympathetically, not cudgelling his brains over it but letting the events themselves work on his feelings, must agree with Loge entirely.'[7] It is possible to sympathise with what Wagner is saying here while feeling that there is still some explaining to be done. For at various stages of *The Ring* statements are made about the consequences of returning the ring whence it came which seem inconsistent.

Puzzlement begins fairly early on: in *The Rhinegold*, when Erda makes her appearance just as Wotan has declared 'The ring stays with me!' she warns him:

> All things that are, perish!
> An evil day
> dawns for the immortals!
> I warn you, yield up the ring!

Wotan understandably wants her to expand on this command but she refuses and Wotan decides, after taking agonised thought, that he will let the giants have the ring. But since Erda's warning was that a dark day was dawning for the gods anyway, it is unclear what finally motivates his action. By the time that he comes, in Act Two of *The Valkyrie*, to tell Brünnhilde what had happened, he has concluded that his present troubles spring partly from his not returning the ring to the Rhinemaidens, though if he had — a point he doesn't make — the giants would not have returned Freia to him. Now he has the problem of getting the ring out of Fafner's grasp without himself

[7] quoted by Newman, *ibid.*

8

committing a further act of violence. But he is caught in two traps: first, the wrong that he did to Alberich could only be undone (if at all) by returning the ring to *him*, which is unthinkable, since Alberich would then rule the world. Secondly, his idea of producing a wholly independent being who, ignorant and innocent, would return the ring to the Rhine has been ruthlessly exposed as sophistry by Fricka in the central moral argument of the whole drama, Wotan's awareness of the insolubility of his dilemma leads him to a great outburst of bitterness, culminating in the cry:

> But one thing I desire:
> the ending,
> that ending!

And yet it seems that even then he hasn't abandoned all hope, for when Waltraute visits Brünnhilde on her rock in Act One of *Twilight*, she tells her sister that Wotan has whispered to her (hence the visit):

> If once the Rhine's fair daughters
> win back their ring from Brünnhild' again
> > then the curse will pass;
> she will save both god and the world!

Brünnhilde refuses, of course, since for her the ring is nothing more nor less than the token of Siegfried's love (a brilliant and painful irony, this, on Wagner's part, to turn the symbol of the denial of love into its opposite, especially in the light of what ensues); she naturally manifests all the exultant egoism of those who are happily in love:

> Love lives in the ring.
> > Go home to the sacred
> > clan of the gods!
> And of my ring
> You may give them this reply:
> My love shall last while I live,
> my ring in life shall not leave me!
> > Fall first in ruins
> Walhall's glorious pride!

She is soon to be proved hideously wrong about how long she will have the ring; nonetheless it is odd that Wotan should still think that 'both god and the world' *would* be saved if it were returned to the Rhine.

With this background of unclarity about what will happen if the ring is returned, it is not surprising that the final scene, during which Brünnhilde does return it, seems to be both ultimately climactic and also confused. Wagner's claim that all will be clear if one simply responds by feeling is valid to the extent that the music of the whole scene is of such transfiguring splendour as to preclude thought at all, at least for the time being. He has achieved an interweaving of motifs so brilliant and so moving, and in the last five minutes a counterpoint of crucial themes which, like all successful counterpoint, seems to have all the rigour of a formal argument, that to raise questions immediately seems merely pusillanimous. Yet not to raise them a decent time afterwards would be to take the work less seriously than it deserves.

The chief beneficiary of the catastrophic events of the earlier part of Act Three of *Twilight* is Brünnhilde herself. We last saw her at the end of Act Two declaring that she had been betrayed by everyone, and that nothing could atone for the wrongs she had suffered, but that she would settle for Siegfried's death; and she proceeded despairingly to join Hagen and Gunther in vowing that it should be effected as soon as possible. Now she is serene and transformed, has come to understand how Siegfried betrayed her, indeed has come, she says, to understand everything. And the state of cosmic enlightenment enables her to invoke peace for Wotan, then to take the decisive step of returning the ring to the Rhinemaidens, and finally to mount Grane and ride with him into Siegfried's pyre. That in her exaltation she still has thoughts of a life beyond death which is not allowed for in the metaphysics of the drama is indicated by her last words (I give a literal translation to make my point clearer):

> Siegfried to embrace,
> embraced by him,
> in mightiest love
> to be wed to him!
> Siegfried! Siegfried!
> Blessedly your wife greets you!

Brünnhilde's delusion here is similar to Isolde's in the last minutes of *Tristan and Isolde*, as she tells the bystanders that she sees Tristan smiling, etc.. But the idea that the union will be a conscious one may be all the more moving for its mistakenness. What is worrying, perhaps, is that in both cases it is an ecstasy in which we, as spectators, share. And we remain exalted as we see (or would do, if producers were to obey Wagner's stage directions) the gods go up in flames in Valhalla. Salvation in Wagner, from *The Flying Dutchman* onwards, is a matter of joyfully embracing annihilation, though at the moment they do so the characters tend to overlook the truth of Wittgenstein's remark that 'Death is not an event in life: we do not live to experience death.' But that their fundamental yearning is a desire not to exist comes out clearly in Wotan's colloquy with Erda in Act Three of *Siegfried*, where, as Wagner put it to Roeckel, 'he rises to the tragic height of willing his own destruction'. What both Wotan and Brünnhilde independently come to realise is that they are parts of an order which is irremediably corrupted; they have tried various ways of undefiling it, but none of them has worked, not even the power of love, which is so often celebrated by many of the chief characters in *The Ring*, but which invariably turns out to be at best disappointing. In the section of Brünnhilde's final address which Wagner didn't set to music, but nonetheless retained when he printed the poem in its final form, she dismisses all ways of being except that of love, without, as Wagner disarmingly wrote to Roeckel, 'unfortunately, making it quite clear what this "love" is which, in the development of the myth, we have seen playing the part of a destroyer.'[8] It was not until his next and last work, *Parsifal*, that Wagner succeeded in fully clarifying the nature of that love which is not destructive, namely compassion, something which Brünnhilde achieves briefly when she apostrophises Wotan and says 'Rest now, rest now, O god!'.

I am not arguing that the final scene of *The Ring* is fully clear or coherent; on the contrary, it manifests tensions which appear in many of Wagner's works in fairly similar forms. On the one hand these astonishing masterpieces demonstrate and can't help celebrating the vitality which is inseparable from

[8] quoted by Newman, *loc. cit.*, p. 354.

Siegmund Nimsgern as Gunther and Hanna Lisowska as Gutrune with Bengt Rundgren as Hagen looming behind, Covent Garden 1976 (photo: Donald Southern)

supreme creativity. On the other hand the central characters are always in search of peace, though in their innermost being they are so deeply divided, and at the same time have such stamina, that only the most shattering experiences can bring them to their deaths. One of the fascinations we find in them, as indeed in their creator, is that they shirk no ordeals in seeking to fulfil themselves. Like the Virgin in Titian's great painting of the Assumption in Venice, which Wagner found such an inspiration, who is 'borne aloft by the fulness of life that is within her' (Berenson's words), they naturally live and die in a state of ecstasy. It is unlikely that most listeners to Wagner's works will feel that they can do the same, but Wagner is hugely invigorating because he makes us realise what it would be like to be like that, in a way that no other artist so consistently does. It's noteworthy that in *Parsifal*, which does not end with the chief characters dying, apart from Kundry, the whole atmosphere of the last act, which makes it unique in Wagner's *oeuvre*, is of a very hard-won but secure peace, in which it *is* possible to imagine continuing to live. The closing pages of his other works suggest that a cycle of existence has been completed, and that even if the characters in them have died from making too great demands on life, as the central characters of *The Ring* certainly do, we can be exhilarated by the insight that Wagner imparts to us through them. It may be that some of that exhilaration comes from the sense we get that we can wipe the slate clean thanks to the thoroughness of the purging. If so, it's as much of a mistake as that idea always is. But reflecting on both the excessiveness and the attraction of Wagner's doomed heroes and heroines may help us, as much as art ever can, to check some impulses in ourselves and encourage others. The sense of enormous potential misdirected is a central

11

feature in all the greatest tragic art, and it is here that Shakespeare and Wagner are most comparable.

So though we may find some aspects of *The Ring* bewildering, apart from the casual inconsistencies which are hardly surprising in a work which occupied its creator for more than a quarter of a century, and find our perplexities most sharply focussed in the final scene, nothing will diminish the impact that it has on us; the comparison with Shakespeare is again inevitable. A response to life from someone who felt so intensely and deeply about as much of it as Wagner did would be suspicious if it issued in something tidy and coherent, and the last bars of *Twilight of the Gods* convey both a sense of the whole tortuous drama being over, but also seem to convey a promise — not one that anybody in the drama survives to fulfil, but one which we, the spectators, are expected to take over and honour. They are Wagner's comment on his vast work, and also an invitation to us not to forget what we have witnessed.

Siegfried's death: Alberto Remedios as Siegfried at ENO, 1976 (photo: Mike Humphrey)

Motif, Memory and Meaning
in 'Twilight of the Gods'

Robin Holloway

No artist has attempted a task more intimidating than Wagner's in writing the last and largest installment of the longest musico-dramatic work yet completed. Coherently but not laboriously to tie up all the threads, to synthesize without artifice, to get the ending absolutely right, required almost superhuman powers. He also made huge demands of his performers in terms of understanding and stamina, of his theatre in technical resources and illusion, and not least of his audience for long-distance concentration upon a drama that unremittingly fuses emotional intensity with dense intellectual argument. Yet he was at pains to make what he is doing at all points self-elucidating. Wagnerian music-drama is mass-communication rather than arcane secret; there are no meaningless ciphers, or inexplicable mysteries; the complex entity glares out with comprehensive exhaustiveness, offering, whatever the depths, a surface that shows everything needed for its own apprehension. It invariably gives the listener a foothold, and sometimes the emphasis of a didactic finger. Tovey's 'first article of musical faith' — that 'while the listener must not expect to hear the whole contents of the piece of music at once, nothing concerns him that will not ultimately reach his ear, either as directly audible fact or as a cumulative satisfaction in things of which the hidden foundations are well and truly laid' — applies as well to Wagner as to the wordless forms which prompted it. How this huge structure works in the small and in the large, how we take in what we hear, how we hear it in the first place, and how we make sense of and interpret it: these are the questions this essay will consider.

They boil down to one: how does Wagner interfuse his music and his meaning? In the large, by his manipulation of musical memory by recapitulations and other formal symmetries, familiar from the music of other periods (though never before so extensive nor so complex); in the small by the leitmotif. Large and small are, of course, closely related. The function of the leitmotif is to build, to describe, to recall. First it gives something a name and a sound; every subsequent incidence is a reminder; at the point when the sound becomes the thing named and we have learned to think in this language, the leitmotif becomes a building-unit from which the structure is formed.

Even at its most straightforward this is not simple. The most purely demonstrative motifs are not one-dimensional, and as the work advances most of them accumulate a web of associations that makes any one name inadequate. An activity (smithying) becomes the whole race of the Nibelungs or an individual Nibelung of particular importance (Mime); an object (his horn) becomes a character (Siegfried). That his sword also comes to 'be' Siegfried is a yet more complex development because we have seen its history — its discovery by his father, the fight in which it was shattered and the father killed, the forge in which it was re-made. With Wotan's spear, the history (slowly divulged, though not seen on the stage, throughout the tetralogy) is such as to make the equation Wotan/spear/authority/contracts/restraints a drastic shorthand whenever the motif is heard. Thus when sword splinters

13

spear in the third act of *Siegfreid*, the cycle reverberates from beginning to end. *Twilight* contains the subtlest example of this process: Alberich's use of the Tarnhelm in *The Rhinegold* is simply to become invisible and to transform himself into serpent and toad; in the first two acts of *Twilight* this fairy-tale device (almost forgotten meanwhile) comes to represent deception, becoming the means whereby deception can be manipulated to play upon an inner weakness. As such it is indispensable to the meaning as well as the mechanism of the plot.

From the most onomatapœic (the waters of the Rhine [1]) to the most abstract (often simply labelled 'destiny', 'renunciation of' — or 'redemption by' — 'love'), the leitmotifs always do their work successfully because they are musical objects of great distinctness. Not only things — objects, places, types, individuals — but activities and ideas, are rendered in brief, memorable *musical things* which scarcely ever change and, when they do, always remain recognisable. As Wagner's paragraphs grow longer, the harmonic usage more supercharged, the motivic combinations (whether fluent or 'yoked together by violence') more bold and subtle, the range of reference further-flung, these essential nuggets can always be apprehended and identified.

Since leitmotifs are memory-containers as well as building-units, the vital facts come to mind whenever the sound is heard. Without this constant reminder of things past we would not be able fully to understand the present. Moreover with leitmotifs memory works forward too; the present is made omniscient by this commentary from fore and aft. 'It takes a sound realist to make a convincing symbolist' (D.J. Enright); the wealth of interpretation *The Ring* attracts would not be possible without its strong basis in specifics.

Take the ring itself. This crucial object has a motif [6] that for once is deliberately not distinct, because the ring is of its nature volatile, amenable to anyone's cupidinous fantasy. But the gold is always present in the ring, and the Rhinemaidens' primal cry of 'Rhinegold!' [4] is remembered whenever the ring motif is heard, whatever the associations and distortions pressed upon it later. By contrast, the motif of the curse placed upon the ring [23] never alters; rather it pulls other motifs into its highly distinctive musical quality, just as it influences everyone's behaviour; equally it recalls at every recurrence what it is, what was said, and how it came about. A curse was pronounced upon a ring made of gold taken from the Rhine; all this is embodied in musical motifs, distinct in themselves yet capable of so intertwining as to make an image-cluster that is finally indissoluble. So much for symbolism! This is the work of a sound realist. It also embodies the drama. The plot could be told from one point of view by following the whereabouts and ownership of the object itself, just as all the occurrences of the curse motif could be joined up to make the 'invisible picture' of Siegfried's death and the fall of the gods. The focus of intense drama in *Rhinegold*, the ring sleeps throughout *The Valkyrie*, comes sharply to mind in the first act of *Siegfried* and into the action of the other two; while in *Twilight* its ownership and whereabouts (whose finger? when? how?) make the clockwork of the story.

Wagner's usual way of working our musical memory hard is intensified in *Twilight* by his extraordinary pains to make salient motifs recur at the same pitch. Sometimes this can even jeopardise musical grammar, though more often it is the stuff of which his grammar is made. Either way there is something almost fetishistic about it, as if the motifs would not have their full significance when transposed. Score-readers and perfect-pitchers will respond to the precision with which the Tarnhelm only seems to work its

14

Above: Therese Malten (Brünnhilde) and Rudolf Milde (Gunther) — a role he sang at Bayreuth in 1896 (Mander and Mitchenson); below, Alois Burgstaller (Siegfried), Bayreuth, 1897, and Heinrich Knote (Siegfried), Covent Garden, 1908 (Royal Opera House Archives)

Some of the singers in the roles they created at Bayreuth in 1876: Georg Unger as Siegfried, Mathilde Weckerlin as Gutrune, Eugen Gura as Gunther and Gustav Siehr as Hagen (Royal Opera House Archives)

treachery when it moves from G# minor through E minor to the bare fifth on B, but this (and the many comparable machinations with other motifs throughout the work) will probably be lost on the great majority of listeners. It is the only aspect of Wagner's method which requires his listeners to hear more than they can reasonably be expected to take in, even while it does form another level, significant because so concrete, in the work's articulation of its meaning. But no-one will fail to recognise what *is* essential: the individuality of each motif's harmony, melody, rhythm, timbre. And the same goes, in a looser way, for Wagner's use of key. Again this is often 'symbolic' — would Siegfried's passing be properly celebrated if his sword were not in C and his horn in E♭? Is Gutrune quite herself except in G? But the main difficulty here comes from the fact that the tonal architecture of *The Ring* is too big to measure. Our key-sense, impressionistic enough even for Haydn and Beethoven, cannot be expected to cope with the more complex tonal activity of Wagner's late style. Yet Tovey's 'first article of musical faith' still applies; we sense that we are in good hands even though it cannot be proved. The broad structure is both simple and rock-hard; within it we concentrate moment-to-moment on the improvisatory riot of detail produced by the leitmotifs and the vagabond modulation to which they are subjected.

The combination of local- (the perpetual play of leitmotivic recall) with memory-architecture on the broadest possible scale (actual recapitulation, developing recapitulation, and parallels of other kinds) together account for the return of all three earlier evenings during the fourth of the tetralogy. By *Twilight*-time our memory is long, and has moreover to accommodate new characters and events, complex and rapid beyond those in any other opera by Wagner, with all the new musical material they necessitate. Its past is richer, its present more intense, and from the very first two chords its end is approaching, inevitable and magnetic, at once louring like a cliff and drawing everything towards it like a cataract. This essay will follow the story as it unrolls forward and refers backward, hanging fast to the means whereby narrative and meaning are fused into music.

*   *   *

The opening chords are taken from Brünnhilde's awakening in the last act of *Siegfried*; the scoring (a massive wind *tutti* yielding to the soft second chord on flutes and low brass) is significantly similar, the effect entirely so; and though we can hardly *hear* that this unforgettable sonorous image now moves from E♭ minor to C♭ major rather than from E minor to C major, we at once connect its two appearances. Moreover the next sound is equally recognisable as a dusky echo of the waters of the Rhine at the very start of the cycle. It is not yet clear what is signified by this gesture that yokes the depths of *Rhinegold* with the summits of *Siegfried*; but it indicates from the start that in *Twilight* our memory of the whole work will be stretched to the limit. It is repeated using the second pair of chords from Brünnhilde's awakening. At the third, when formerly the light shone brightest, the blast of E♭ minor sinks into the fate-motif [38], and what follows is not the river again but a cobweb of soft shifting dissonance [62] — the Norns, a trio of nature-daughters as old, withered and wise as the Rhinemaidens are young, fresh and foolish. Their scene is build around the refrain spinning the rope of fate [63] which functions as a kind of *ritornello* while they tell by question-and-answer of events already known and events hitherto unheard; thus many old themes are called to mind in ashy guise (particularly the strange slowed-down version of the fire music, formerly so volatile), as the basis for their look into the future.

The three Norns: Patricia Payne, Linda Finnie and Pauline Tinsley at Covent Garden in the Götz Friedrich production, desig·:ed by Josef Svoboda with costumes by Ingrid Rosell, 1978 (photo: Reg Wilson)

We learn for the first time the history of the World Ash-Tree: how Wotan violated it to win his wisdom and his spear by paying an eye, how the deed wasted the tree and dried up its spring of wisdom. We learn again of the hero who splintered the spear and every treaty it upheld; we learn newly of Wotan's consequent command to fell the dead tree and pile its logs around Valhalla ready for razing should the moment come. We discover new angles of Wotan's relation to Loge, and how the god will command the fire to ignite the logs as once he compelled him to encircle Brünnhilde. Seeking to know what happened to the stolen gold the Norns hear only the echo of Alberich's cry for revenge; a bright horn-call cuts through their cobwebs, the rope connecting past and future snaps, and, as the curse sounds for the first time in *Twilight*, they sink from sight, their wisdom spent.

The curse [23] suggests a cadence into B minor. The famous dawn-music that follows lingers suspiciously long upon the dominant, but the F♯ inaudibly turns to G♭ which descends to F over which Siegfried's horn-call sounds forth [64], soft, but with grand full harmony like a chorale, in B♭ major. The new dominant bass also lasts too long for credibility: as a new motif flowers (65 — the motif of Brünnhilde's fulfilment in love) the tonality turns decisively towards E♭ major, though even now there are still 17 more bars of dominant preparation before the sun rises with the sun-god's horn theme in full splendour. The lavish radiance of the duet that follows makes its maximum contrast with the shadowy impotence of the Norns by the simplest of all key-relationships, major to minor. Yet it, also, is a reworking of old themes in a new light, built upon a *ritornello* figure [66] which frames and punctuates the lovers' almost formal apostrophes to each other before

The three Norns: Anna Maragaki, Roswitha Fischer and Margarete Ast in the 1974 production at the State Theatre, Kassel, produced by Ulrich Melchinger and designed by Thomas Richter Forgach.

pervading everything in the rapturous close. This technique of building a scene around a *ritornello* motif seems to be unique to the later *Ring* style: the first instance, using the second half of [55], is the dialogue between Erda and the Wanderer that opens the third act of *Siegfried*; it is employed throughout *Twilight*, whether with explicit refrain as with the Norns, or subtly incorporated into a texture of continuous development.

Siegfried, going out into the world as a man has to, innocently gives Brünnhilde the ring as a love-pledge. She gives him Grane in return. The scene ends in a blaze of E♭ major glory which links across the intervening space to the next 'mountain-top', the climax of the interlude describing his journey, the marvellous moment of liberation when he sees the Rhine lying broad and clear in its valley far beneath. This is no less a *coup-de-théâtre* even if the curtain is down. We have not seen the river after *The Rhinegold*. The motifs of its waters and its treasure [1c, 4] have become steadily more smirched, and the most recent re-hearing, in the Norn scene, had rendered them thin and lacklustre. So the thrill of this restoration of the river's motifs to their pristine freshness and their primal key is achieved purely by sonorous means, which then ramify into broader interpretative significance. Siegfried is in the flower of his youth and innocence; he won the ring in fair fight, not lusting for it, and ignorant of its possibilities; he has given it to his lady to pledge his love. These twin peaks of E♭ major are the work's high-points of optimism. The darkening of the *Rhinegold*-cry as the interlude ends, and the way it turns subtly but purposefully into the first Gibichung motif, tell us unmistakably that the rest of the journey will be ill-fated.

The Prologue has been made almost entirely from familiar material richly reworked. The main action is set in a new place among new characters, the Gibichung court and its troubled first family. This necessitates new material [68-70, 72-75] whose chivalric cast reminds us that *Siegfried's Death*, the *Ring* project as first mooted, would have been Wagner's next opera after *Lohengrin* (1849) rather than, as it turned out, the sixth. But this new material is permeated by the old, just as the new characters have inherited old memories and desires. The basic key is B minor, into which the curse that ended the Norns' scene would have cadenced were it not deflected by dawn, duet and Siegfried's journey. And just as the Rhine runs alongside the action for the rest of the work, so is the curse motif never far from the music, because Hagen knows that Siegfried holds the woman who holds the ring that holds the curse. (How does Hagen know? With hindsight we understand that his ever-watchful father keeps him in touch in the way we will overhear for ourselves in the first scene of Act Two.)

The way the old motifs function in new situations shows the possibilities raised by Wagner's methods at their boldest, achieving complex dramatic expression that words have to labour to explain. Hagen's newly-planted idea takes root, that the Gibichungs use Siegfried to solve their troubles: he can marry Gutrune and win Brünnhilde for Gunther. 'How can we bring him here?' asks Gunther, and the curse arises from the orchestra pit intertwined with Siegfried's horn-call from down the river. A moment later Hagen describes his progress — 'with a powerful stroke, / yet with leisurely ease, / he drives the boat, / braving the stream.' The music is now the *Rhinegold*-cry and the flowing river itself, crossed with Siegfried's horn, the whole image-cluster fused into a graphic description of the hero's muscular prowess ('such strength in his arms / . . . it is he who destroyed the [dragon]. / Siegfried's coming, he and no other'.) Another moment, and Siegfried is near enough to hear and answer Hagen's call; another, and he appears, lands, and is greeted by name with courteous words. But they are set to a lurid, rhetorical statement of the curse-motif, with upbeat drumstrokes and climactic cymbal crash, the loudest sound in the work so far — though its presentation is the reverse of those twin peaks of sustained brilliance the end of the love duet and the climax of the river-journey: it arises rapidly out of *pianissimo*, diminishes immediately after maximum impact, and soon collapses into complete silence when Siegfried, his future bride, brother-in-law and slayer confront each other in electric embarrassment. The implication is so large as to make this moment architectural rather than local, a turning-point in the drama as a whole. Siegfried's arrival is desired, brooded upon, broached, agreed; at just the right moment the music brings him up the river in person; and here he will meet his death because the music says so. The words here are simply the necessary formalities; the leitmotif tells the truth. Although the ring itself is distant, such musical emphasis compels us to remember the curse's origin (often forgotten as the motif comes and goes on less crucial occasions) in the words Alberich burned into his treasure as he lost it; they have never failed so far, and they will not fail as the decisive first move is made in the game by which its noblest victim will be taken. Here the motif denotes the fulfilment of Alberich's ultimate ambition, the downfall of the gods, and names Siegfried as the instrument of this fulfilment. The importance of this conjunction is confirmed by the emphatic move back into the temporarily forgotten B minor effected by the curse-motif's being at its usual pitch.

This mighty moment is followed by its echo, as Siegfried asks Hagen how he knows his name (whose two syllables are again set to the curse's falling octave). This time the crucial dissonance (23, fifth bar, always over a pedal F#) alters and the music moves into the unctuous warmth of the Gibichungs' deceptive cordiality [74]. The curse's next occurrence confirms that events are indeed moving with dream-like ease. Through the reverse-side of his innocence and courage — his inexperience of men and their ways, his ignorance of himself — Siegfried is easily tricked into drinking Gutrune's magic drink. Within minutes he has agreed to fetch Brünnhilde for Gunther in exchange for that standard item of barter, the sister; and his new cunning suggests how the Tarnhelm can help. Before Hagen explained, he didn't know what the Tarnhelm was for. Now — another instance of the rich compression of meaning made possible by the leitmotif — he has drunk self-deception with the potion of forgetfulness that represents it in a stage-prop (71 shows the original Tarnhelm motif [18] extended into deception of others and of self). So when the curse begins and ends the oath of blood-brotherhood between Siegfried and Gunther [69] we understand quite explicitly that this brew of heartiness and harshness provides permission and justification for Siegfried's death, when occasion offers, uttered freely by his own words — 'If one friend should betray, / then not drops of blood, / all his life blood — / shall flow in streams from his veins; / traitors so must atone!'

Doped and duped, Siegfried sets off eagerly back the way he came, to win for his new blood-brother the woman he has already won for himself. Hagen keeps watch, developing the dark choked harmony peculiar to *Twilight* into a brooding set-piece that, with the *Rhinegold*-cry in a piercingly dissonant harmonisation —

Example A

— makes a transition to Siegfried's goal, Brünnhilde's rock, where she awaits his second coming. We hear the curse now entwined with fragments of her new love-theme [65] as the action again nears the accursed object, worn on her finger. Instead of what she wants to hear, 'sounds (she) once knew so well steal on (her) ears from the distance' as her Valkyrie sister Waltraute approaches. We know them too; the sisters' scene together brings back the essence of Act Three of *Valkyrie*, Wotan's rage at his errant daughter, together with the music from Act Two when, while she was still obedient, he told her his dilemma. It moves on to Waltraute's full-scale description of what the Norns have already touched on: the Ash-Tree cut down and piled in logs around Valhalla and the vast hall thronged with silent heroes awaiting the unknown outcome. This superb set-piece gives the basis for the apotheosis of Valhalla in the closing pages of *Twilight*; while the music for the description of Wotan speechlessly clutching his shattered spear, for the raven-messengers who will return with good news or ill, and for the words eventually wrung from him as he remembers his love for Brünnhilde ('If once the Rhine's fair daughters / win back their ring from Brünnhilde again, / then the curse will pass; / she will save both god and the world!') — all separated here by Waltraute's account of the frightened gods deprived of Freia's apples, the

Gwyneth Jones as Brünnhilde and Yvonne Minton as Waltraute, Covent Garden, 1978 (photo: Reg Wilson)

Valkyries cowering at their father's knee, and her own temerity in persuading Wotan at last to speak — are worked into the sublime continuous stretch of the last scene where Brünnhilde, at last understanding everything, tells the ravens what they need to know and grants the god his quietus. Here is another turning-point of the work, requiring references backward and forward and marked by a fusion of gold, curse and ring motifs, working towards a full-close in the Valhalla music in its first and last key of D♭. If Brünnhilde had not been told *now*, when she is least likely to yield it, what ought to be done with the ring, she would not know what to do with it after the catastrophe.

But *now* she holds fast to her love-pledge, Waltraute rushes off in despair, and Brünnhilde remains alone surrounded by flames as at the end of *Valkyrie*; except that she is awake, her rescuer has come, and the music tells her of his unexpected return. Siegfried's second ascent through the flames is an exact repetition of his first in *Siegfried* Act Three; where it diverges, in the horrible dissonant chord at the climax, it points the crucial difference: that it is not Siegfried. The chord is the dominating harmony of Hagen's Watch (still in progress, of course); Brünnhilde sees Gunther's form, and we (as Hagen's chord collapses onto the start of the Tarnhelm motif) see a Siegfried who is directed by Hagen and no longer his own man.

Both legitimate owners are close to the ring. Brünnhilde cries that so long as she wears it safe (if only she could heed the *music* to which her own words are set, she would know they couldn't be true — but, unlike Siegfried, she is still unaware of the Tarnhelm's power to deceive). Siegfried, singing the curse as a melodic contour (unusual in itself) says 'from you I shall take it / taught by your words!' and a scuffle ensues, beginning with Hagen's hideous *Rhinegold*-cry, then fought out between her own motif and the curse. The

22

curse wins as Siegfried gains his own love-pledge; again a raucous sound collapses into the Tarnhelm motif, through whose miasma she unconsciously looks into and recognises Siegfried's eyes. He, having done this foul deed as blithely as he once dispatched a dragon, now calls upon his sword to lie between them in the cave, keeping his new bride inviolate for his brother [79]. It is important that Brünnhilde, in all the wretchedness of her betrayal, hears this music; in her final monologue she will return to this unwittingly false oath sworn upon a true touchstone, explain it, and put it right. The act ends with the Tarnhelm motif *tutta forza* at its usual pitch: the note B runs through all its three chords, grounding the entire Gibichung act in a B minor whose sway has been potent though its periods in office have been brief.

*   *   *

The prelude to Act Two is the continuation of Hagen's Watch from Act One, making from the same ingredients the harshest music in all Wagner (see example A). The scene it introduces, between Hagen as he sleeps and his never-resting father Alberich, is another prologue, like the Norn-scene both retelling old matters and glimpsing future events by now equally familiar. But whereas the Norn-music had moved slowly enough to be grasped readily, the motifs are here broken down and recombined in a style of rapid allusive lightness that makes this the most difficult area of *The Ring* to assimilate. Furthermore, Alberich's angle on the familiar makes it different. Wotan's defeat at Siegfried's hands, and his preparations for the end, the hero's blithe lordship of the ring making its curse ineffective: this well-covered territory is now whispered in hectic consternation — only Siegfried's undoing can win it for them: 'he's a fool, the real enemy is the wisdom of the woman he's won — if

Alberto Remedios as Siegfried disguised by the Tarnhelm as Gunther at ENO (photo: John Garner)

Bengt Rundgren as Hagen and Zoltan Kelemen as Alberich in the Centenary cycle at Covent Garden, 1976 (photo: Donald Southern)

she has the wit to return ring to Rhine our hopes are ended.' Between these flustered utterances come Hagen's stolid assurances that, he, too, works what his father desires.

We learn the history of Hagen (already hinted in *The Valkyrie* Act Two) from its source — how Alberich begot and reared his son in hatred to accomplish what his father cannot do for himself. Thus we understand why Hagen looms so large in the meaning as well as the mechanics of the plot. Hagen is far closer to Siegfried than are either to Gunther (respectively half-brother and relation by oath and, later today, marriage): both have been conceived to fulfil the aims of others, have grown autonomous and revolted against their manipulators; they are brothers under the skin. As the scene closes with both phrases of the curse (in honour of him who first uttered it)

Hagen tranquilly quietens his father's anxiety with the assurance that he swears to himself, and to no other, that he will gain the ring. Here too he stands apart; the cupidity in the ring breeds betrayal even when father and son share a mutual end. For Alberich is clearly not up-to-date, and Hagen has made no attempt to tell him that what he desires is already in motion, that his shadow-brother, though defying dragon and Wotan head-on, can be manipulated from behind.

Twilight had begun with a re-creation of the opening of *Rhinegold*. Now comes a second, a dawn over the Rhine which, like the dawn dissolving the remnants of the Norns when their rope broke, dissolves the memory of Alberich, making the colloquy seem like Hagen's dream before the day that will see the fruition of his plans. This 'dawn-chorus' evokes the opening of *Rhinegold* by sonority and texture; over a Bb pedal a flowing canon for the eight horns rises, with a new thematic contour that provides material for the first part of the main action [83]. Most of the other Act Two music is familiar, but the curse motif undergoes a striking evolution. Hitherto it has been the quintessential 'musical thing'; now its separate elements, so tightly locked into each other, pull apart and go against each other, the musical grammarian in Wagner working with the dramatist to elicit the full extent of its latent power. Hagen's set-piece summoning the Gibichung vassals shows soon enough the enormous musical charge released when the curse is detonated. His uncouth epic jocularity stems on the surface from his saturnine humour ('Glad times have come to our Rhine, / when Hagen, / grim Hagen, / with laughter can shine!') and underneath from his satisfaction at the speed with which his purpose is ripening. Having seen to it that Brünnhilde is already wronged, he can vindicate the deed that he does for his own interest as if it were a communal good. 'Honour your lady, / come to her aid; / if she is wronged, / you must revenge her.'

These dark strains are temporarily forgotten in the magnificent chorus of welcome, its Bb major answering the Bb minor of the Hagen/Alberich scene just as the Eb major of Brünnhilde, Siegfried and the Rhine illuminated the Norns' Eb minor in the Prologue to Act One. Those who remember Brünnhilde's vulnerability after her first rapture of awakening in *Siegfried* Act Three will catch its momentary reappearance here as she stands mute, with eyes downcast, between the first huge burst of greeting and Gunther's ceremonial words. After a second blast of vassals, Gunther continues in warm, florid periods somewhat reminiscent of old Nuremberg, culminating in the four names of the participants in the double wedding. Last comes Siegfried, and Brünnhilde is galvanised. A motif first heard in the wretched manœuvres at the end of Act One, then worried in and out of Alberich's anxiety at the start of this act, now assumes great prominence for the rest of the action [78]. She nearly faints — 'My eyes grow dim . . .' and Siegfried, who once kissed them awake, rushes to support her. She looks into his face, as when he was disguised by the Tarnhelm; he betrays no recognition; but on his finger she recognises what betrays him — 'Ha! The ring — / upon his hand! / He . . Siegfried?' (and its curse rises in the orchestra). 'Now mark her words', says Hagen when the squalid and inexplicable muddle is exposed. To music first heard in *Rhinegold* as Alberich conceived the curse, which then return as, having uttered it, he spells out its inevitable consequences [22], she presses her bewilderment — 'A ring I see / upon *your* hand; / that ring was stolen, / it was taken / seized by *him*! / So how did you gain / that ring from his hand?' Siegfried remains unperturbed: *'absorbed in distant thoughts while con-*

25

templating the ring', his fuddled memory permits a beautiful glimpse into his past, when he fought the dragon and gained the ring — briefly the gold motif is heard pure as the time of his boyish valour is recalled. Then, in a fine motif-pun, Hagen takes the 'dragon' tritone away from territory where Siegfried might remember too much, and forces confusion into confrontation: 'Brünnhild, are you sure /you recognise the ring? / For if it is Gunther's ring, / if it is his, / then Siegfried was false to his friend; / he must pay then for his treachery!' He is premature; even if true this would be too petty a misdeed to justify to the onlookers the vengeance he wants; he cannot understand that Brünnhilde's betrayal is on a higher plane than a wrangle for a ring. She cries out to the gods at the outrage (Hagen's version of the *Rhinegold*-call, Example A, and the ubiquitous ring motif itself) — let them teach her such vengeance as never was, let her heart be broken, so long as he who broke it atones.

A sudden phrase of conventional rant, cadencing a paragraph of high inspiration, occurs as she makes her cataclysmic announcement that she is already Siegfried's wife. This creaking flaw is soon forgotten in the battle of wits that now begins. It is her word against his; the details of their night together emerge; Gunther realises the extent of his shame if she is not refuted; Gutrune, Siegfried's; the men take up the cry to resolve it by oath. 'Which of you warriors will lend me his spear?' asks Siegfried. This is now the right moment for Hagen; the killer and his weapon are ready for the hero to confirm his unknowing falseness and assure his own death. This vital moment in the plot is not articulated by the music as a great turning-point like Hagen's first greeting to Siegfried in Act One — which we now realise, is powerful enough to reverberate on to the moment of its fulfilment in Act Three. Here the pace is so fast that we sail straight into the next set-piece: rival oaths sworn on

Act Two of Patrice Chéreau's Bayreuth production, designed by Richard Peduzzi with costumes by Jacques Schmidt, with Gwyneth Jones as Brünnhilde and Franz Mazura as Gunther, 1978 (photo: Festspielleitung Bayreuth)

26

The oath on the spear in Act Two of the 1974 production at Kassel with, from left to right, Béla Turpinszki as Siegfried, Martin Matthias Schmidt as Gunther, Fraugiskos Voutsinos as Hagen, Joy McIntyre as Brünnhilde and Carmen Reppel as Gutrune.

Hagen's willing spear. Siegfried says, (*lit.*) 'If I am to be slain for treachery, let this be the weapon.' Brünnhilde says (*lit.*) 'Let this be the weapon by whose point he dies, for he has broken all his vows.' Their vocal contours are almost identical but the rhythmic values differ greatly, and her orchestra, as well as a fierce Valkyrie fizzing, produces an echoing trumpet-line, only hinted at before. Her version expands, and finally she sings more than he, and more vehemently. He is drugged and has no idea of what is really happening; she knows that she has lost everything worth having and desires his death. Now they have both uttered this thought, Hagen only needs to work it round to word, then deed. The crazed intensity of the whole scene erupts as the men call upon the gods' thunder to drown the disgrace. This diffuses the turmoil; Siegfried manages to pass the events off lightly, promising a good outcome and leading everyone off to the wedding-feast.

The curse, silent since Brünnhilde saw the ring on the wrong hand, closes a scene of maximum turbulence with architectural punctuation, as if to guarantee that it governs what has been witnessed and what will now follow. Hagen, Gunther and Brünnhilde join forces to activate it (the ring is still on Siegfried's finger as he carouses nearby). Even at the height of the turmoil Brünnhilde was able to unscramble part of the confusion; now her mother-wit shows her further that Siegfried was disguised, that Hagen was somehow responsible, that Gutrune was the bait. But this partial realisation only exacerbates, and Hagen is able to elicit from her rage and grief what her love would never admit: that Siegfried can be struck down from the back. Another vital hinge in the mechanism, this time not sailed over, but instead deliberately underplayed and even contradicted. For the music here recalls him as the 'child of delight' from their duet in *Siegfried* Act Three [58] and the love-music from the Prologue of *Twilight* [66]; her pride in his courage that will never turn its back to a foe is the first intimation that by the end of the work her love for him will have ousted her hate. These ambiguities do not interest Hagen, who now has all he needs — 'My spear knows where to strike!' — and turns to the next item, taunting Gunther till he too will acquiesce. Brünnhilde also rounds upon him. His cry for help in an anguish of shame at last provokes the *words* for what has been fixed by the music since Hagen hailed Siegfried with the curse — *Siegfried's Death*, Wagner's earliest title, remains a more accurate focus upon the work's central event than the mythological distancing of his final choice. Hagen dares utter them; Gunther dully questions; Brünnhilde flares up in confirmation — 'So the death of one / now must content me: / Siegfried's death / atones for his crime, and yours!' So Hagen has to tempt Gunther with the ring. Gunther sighs over his new blood-brother's fate and his sister's unhappiness, but the curse's poison (*lit.* 'all who see it shall desire it, and it shall give them no joy') quickly works. Brünnhilde, thus reminded of the poor creature, spits out her hatred of Gutrune; Hagen devises the details of how Siegfried may plausibly be killed; and when Gunther next speaks he has agreed — 'It shall be so! / Siegfried dies then!' All three sing together to their various gods of their common aim; Gunther and Brünnhilde to Wotan that he witness the broken oath and the just revenge, Hagen to the lord of the Nibelungs that the oppressed race shall soon once more obey their ring-master. The music is a riot of the new material in Acts One and Two, especially the two oaths, the first act's as prominent as the second's, permeated by the dissonance released by splitting the curse motif. When the smouldering trio yields to the marriage festivities that end the act, this split creates its most powerful effect since the vassals were summoned; the C major triad of its fifth bar makes loud specious merriment, but its tonic and dominant are assaulted simultaneously with tritonal and semitonal clashes from F$\sharp$ and D$\flat$ — Alberich and Hagen uniting to overthrow consonance and stability.

*   *   *

Act Three is entirely based upon familiar material and, as the work moves towards its end, explicit evocation of its past increases, amounting in one instance to a section of pure repetition, though wonderfully recast for its new context. Almost at once, after Siegfried's and the Gibichung's hunting-horns have resounded from all sides and the curse-harmony recalled the hunt's secret purpose, comes the third and most direct return to the start of *Rhinegold*; eight horns rise from the depths in canon in their fundamental notes, crowned in the tenth bar by the *Rhinegold*-call in its freshest diatonic form. What had originally taken 113 pages of orchestral score is here encapsulated in 15 bars! When the Rhine-music resumes after a further salvo of horn-calls, it is different, coloured by delicate, melancholy chromaticism as the girls sing of the dark waters that were once bright with their gold. They cheer up at the prospect of the hero who will restore the ring, knowing who he is and that he is near. As his horn sounds closer they dive down to take counsel, and Siegfried appears on the bank, puzzled, led astray by an elusive quarry. The gold's guardians reappear, and it is clear from their words that they have arranged the encounter. They try to tease him into giving them the ring, but fail; he refuses them what they long for too much. Left alone he reflects — they had called him miserly, teased him for being too answerable to

28

his wife; he takes off the ring, holds it high, and calls to them that they can have it. But they also have changed their tactics; he can keep it, and taste the ill fate that it carries. Unafraid, he returns it to his finger, asking them to tell what they know. And now their solemn warnings are useless; no more than they could tease it can they force it from him, though they screech his name to Hagen's piercing version of the *Rhinegold*-call. They tell him what we know so well but he not at all. Singing the curse in unison they become portentous as Norns, and when he is not swayed they almost turn into their faded sisters, reproducing, to frighten him, first Erda's warning from *Rhinegold*, then the Norns' web of fate. Siegfried is contemptuous and superb — (*lit.*) 'My sword once shattered a spear; if a curse is woven into the web of fate, I'll cut the Norns asunder!' This accidental reference to a point where his memory is blocked elicits from the still-callow Siegfried, who has only the day before rushed into false relations and sold his true wife up the river, a moment of reflective gravity: 'Though Fafner once warned me / to flee the curse / yet he could not teach me to fear. / The world's wealth / I could win me by this ring: / for a glance of love / I would exchange it; / if you had smiled the ring would be yours. / But you threatened my limbs and my life: / now though the ring / had no worth at all, (*lit.* not worth a finger) / you'd still not get it from me. / My limbs and my life! — / See! So freely I'd fling it away!' (as he 'picks up a clod of earth, holds it high over his head, and throws it away behind him').

By their ill-judged babbling, the Rhinemaidens have lost their treasure all over again when it was so close to home. Their consternation at his astonishing words shows that, for all their prescience, they have not foreseen the outcome their behaviour has ensured, though they know what will happen after he has decided so wrongly. But is he wrong? It is not clear whether this is a moment of supreme freedom for Siegfried, or whether he is still bound, for all his brave words, in the web of fate. The rules of the story say that he is not free to return the gold; the ring is not yet cleansed, and he who wears it carries its curse. But Siegfried, uninterested in the ring's limitless powers, using it only as a love-pledge for Brünnhilde, is untouched by the causes that animated the curse. And it is not until this scene that he has ever understood what he was playing with. Fafner told him of the curse as he died by it, but Siegfried was hot from the fight and longing to learn from the dying creature only about himself. The woodbird told him that the ring would make him master of the world. Neither dragon nor bird connected ring with curse; and when Siegfried emerged from the cave bearing ring and Tarnhelm on the bird's advice, one of the most beautiful passages in the cycle described his regret that these pretty toys were useless in teaching him to fear.*

The truth is that Siegfried's guilt with regard to the ring is of a different kind from everyone else's. He has never desired the power and wealth it bestows. On the contrary he is 'the world's treasure' who makes power and wealth seem paltry. But he has wrested it by force from the woman to whom he gave it freely as the symbol of their love, and so negated that love. Where Siegfried is concerned, the intertwined curse and ring come to *mean* something different. What Alberich had renounced to get the gold, Siegfried had placed in the gold; what Alberich had 'sublimated' shines forth in

---

* When we remember what *did* teach him fear we realise that this is a delicate moment in the mechanism, as well as the meaning, of *Twilight* as a whole. If Siegfried can recall breaking Wotan's spear, why not also what he was so impatient to reach when the spear barred his way to it? Perhaps, the main deception-work being done, his memory is beginning to return even before it is prompted.

Siegfried as pure libido. The gold has Siegfried's life-force within it; the ring freely given is his loving virility, the ring forcibly wrested destroys both Brünnhilde and himself. The scene where he teases the Rhinemaidens with the gold makes a titillating echo of these high themes. In this way the curse applies to a hero who, although innocent of greed, is inherently vulnerable. Hagen knew his man's weakness before Brünnhilde confessed to his unprotected back, when he induced Siegfried to desire Gutrune. 'Dayspring mishandled cometh not again.' The ring comes to stand for what in Siegfried can so readily betray Brünnhilde. It is therefore accursed for him too, and Alberich's words on it must still come true: 'To death he is fated, doomed by the curse on the ring!' (The symbolism of the ring and its curse is at its most complex here, so Wagner, sound realist that he is, ensured that for once the object itself can be seen quite clearly by everyone, on stage and in the theatre!)

Moreover it would be out of character for Siegfried to give the ring back to the Rhine. It would be weak, prudent, ignoble, rather than impetuous, youthful, proud. Alternatively, it would be more 'grown-up' than Siegfried has shown himself so recently to be. He is still something of a bold booby like Parsifal at his first appearance, with a long journey towards full humanity before him, cut off almost before it *has* begun. That it has begun, this vacillation over the ring and the gravity that underlies the bravado of his words attest. Though overflowing with life (especially on this his last day) he seems not to mind dying, and will of course face it fearlessly. 'I value myself little and freely fling away this valueless thing' — there is profound complexity in the image-cluster of the 'finger's-worth' of his life: the ring on his finger, the life-force in the ring, the clod of earth that like himself he can freely cast into extinction, and the gold that, whatever it means, he holds up high yet does not fling away. Irrespective of what he now chooses to decide with the Rhinemaidens, his death is already sealed: the oaths on Hagen's spear, the trio with the declared aim of Siegfried's death, and assassin, weapon and occasion all worked out. There is moreover a death-premonition and acquiescence in Siegfried himself that resonates remarkably with the wider course of the cycle as a whole. It is the death-wish of the unmorbid animal in full flush of youth and spirits: a fair animal hunted by a black shadow that finds the one place which is weak, soft, rotten, connected with what first taught fear — 'My spear knows where to strike!'

The answer from the *music* is that this is not one of the work's secret but mighty hinges. It is certainly dense and elliptical in its combination of leitmotifs; Siegfried's most complex musical moment, in striking contrast to the directness of the narrative in the following scene. His words to the Rhinemaidens are best taken as generous overflow, like his still grander bravado, still closer to death, when the wine he drinks with his murderers spills over onto the earth and he hails the universal mother — that earth which he threw over his shoulder and into which his blood will soon soak in a still more generous libation. Ardent, abundant, glorious even when technically both traitor and dupe, he amply justifies Brünnhilde's final exoneration of his heroism.

Apart from this, what would become of the rest of the story if he returned the gold to the Rhinemaidens? And Brünnhilde? He *is* caught in the mesh of past and future, as he is caught in the flaws of his own character. Still a mixture of Rhinemaidens and old Norns, the girls thrash the waters in violent agitation, seeing present ('He thinks he is wise, / he thinks he is strong, / but he's stupid and blind as a child!') and future ('your ring returns to

The Rhinemaidens with Siegfried in (above) the Chéreau production, 1979 and (below) the Peter Hall production, designed by William Dudley, 1984, at Bayreuth (photos: Festspielleitung Bayreuth)

Noel Mangin as Hagen, Alberto Remedios as Siegfried and Norman Welsby as Gunther in Act Three of the ENO production in 1976 (photo: Mike Humphrey)

Brünnhilde, / by her, our prayer will be heard') for what they are and will be. 'To her!' they cry in turn, their last intelligible syllables. Suddenly the music turns radiant and stable again; they sing their perennial *Weialala* tinged with *Twilight* melancholy, but fresh as if they had not a care in the world. Siegfried too is happy. He smiles as he sings of the ways of women. Were it not for his troth to Gutrune he'd surely have enjoyed one of these delicious water-creatures! As their voices, then their music, disappear, the curse closes the scene with architectural punctiliousness, restoring 'Hagen-harmony', above which the Gibichung horns approach and Siegfried answers with his own. The next time we will hear the curse motif is the moment when Hagen strikes him down.

The hunting-party now joins him beside the river. The music is made of lusty diatonic materials — Gibichung music and Siegfried's horn-calls — presented with bucolic roughness; but its latent unease sounds in 'Hagen-harmony' when Siegfried tells them that his death has been foretold for that very day. He alone remains blithe and genial.

The course of *Twilight*, while moving fast through a new and complex story, has managed to bring before us the events and music of almost every salient part of the three preceding operas. Now comes the simplest and most wonderful return, of the long epoch when Brünnhilde was asleep; the boyhood of her deliverer, covering the action of the first two acts of *Siegfried*. It comes neither in the form of a web of allusion like the Norns, nor a reiteration of old obsessions like Alberich; appropriately for Siegfried, it is pure narration. But his memory is blocked. We have heard him recall how he gained the ring, and that his sword once shattered a spear. Between these and

32

beyond them his memory has to be prompted and stage by stage unlocked. A beautiful three-note motif [88] does this; it is Siegfried's *madeleine*, a horn-motif, turning upon itself over tenderly shifting harmony, speaking of nostalgia for time lost, showing that this 'overjoyous' man of action, as Gunther calls him, begins again to reflect and look within himself as he had as a boy when his life lay still before him. Thus it is also the motif of his dawning awareness: as more of his experience is allowed, he possesses himself more fully; land reclaimed from the drugged past and understood for the first time. Finally he repossesses Brünnhilde too. He has grown again to his full stature, a man as great as the woman he awoke or the god he pushed aside. But by the same token this self re-possession also means his death, since in his progress towards illumination he will inevitably reveal what will lead to his murder.

It begins simply. When Siegfried says lightly that some waterbirds have told him he will be killed today, Gunther and Hagen exchange dark looks. Hagen passes it off — 'A cruel and evil hunt, / if the bear should get away, / and then a boar should kill you!' — and Siegfried passes on; 'I'm thirsty' and the memory -motif makes its first appearance. Hagen prompts: (*lit*.) 'Can it be true you understand birdsong?' but Siegfried is not yet tempted; he boisterously exchanges drinking horns with his downcast blood-brother, mingles the wine so that his overflows, and dedicates the offering to mother-earth. Gunther gloomily calls him 'overjoyous' and Siegfried jokes aside to Hagen that Brünnhilde must be causing trouble. Hagen keeps him to the point — 'Her voice is not so clear / as the song of birds to you!' But Siegfried does not react; the memory-motif as yet only recalls waterbirds and woodbird — 'Since women have sung their songs to me, / I've cared for the birdsong no more.' Hagen and motif persist — 'Yet once you knew it well?' — and though he does not immediately get what he pursues, his insistent hints surely contribute to the overflow when it comes.

Immediately, however, Siegfried attempts to enliven Gunther and the gloomy party with tales of his boyhood. Here there is no ban; his memory has been gently stirred, making it natural enough for him to begin at the beginning and continue till he can advance no further. The nostalgia-motif turns its contour towards Mime's forging music as formal introduction. Once started, Siegfried moves quickly to recall the 'starling-song' of the dwarf's self-pity at the boy's ingratitude, how he was reared to achieve Mime's ambition — to kill the dragon and gain the gold for him who couldn't, how he forged anew from its splinters his father's sword, how they found the place, and how with the sword he killed Fafner the foe. It is quite uncanny how Wagner in two pages of vocal score captures in fluent flashback the audible essence of enormous tracts of previous music. Now the pace slows. 'Now you must hear / what happened next: / wondrous things I can tell you.' They all return: the dragon's blood ('and when the blood / had but wetted my tongue', the motif is there, now on oboe and english horn, prompting both memory and understanding, hinting at the thematic contour of the sleeping woman [43] in anticipation of what cannot yet be *licitly* recalled); Mime's self-revealing plot, his death, and Siegfried's wondering possession of ring and Tarnhelm. Such is the spate of recall he has not needed prompting; he relives his past in the present, as if the bird spoke to him now or even spoke through him, making clear again things that have since become opaque. But after Mime's death there is the expected hiatus; Hagen's coarse jest ('unable to forge it, still he could feel it!', exactly reproducing his father's Nibelung-laughter at the moment the dwarf had been killed) nearly breaks the spell. Now two vassals take up the prompting —

33

'What heard you then from the woodbird?' and again the *madeleine* (now restored to the french horn) gently insinuates its three notes and a very expressive fourth. It is this subtle musical elicitation that makes his access to the next events of his adventures so credible, rather than the mere mechanics of the new potion squeezed by Hagen into his wine. 'Drink first, hero, / from my horn. / I have here a noble drink; / let its freshening power wake your remembrance.' Siegfried looks deep into the horn and drinks slowly; the besottedness in Act One is audibly reversed; strangled sounds of Tarnhelm yield to a tender, infinitely remote memory of Brünnhilde, not as he first knew her in *Siegfried* but in their rapture at the start of *Twilight*. This tiny glimpse of the later work in what is otherwise a recall only of the earlier has an effect moving out of all proportion to its size.

He has freed himself to release what happened next. 'In grief I watched / the branches above'; the woodbird's comforting advice for his loneliness — the glorious bride sleeping surrounded by flames, and how she can be won — out it all comes. Once Brünnhilde's name is uttered, Gunther listens in horrified astonishment. Hagen's next cue ('and did you take / the woodbird's counsel?') is scarcely needed, for Siegfried's rapturous recollection cannot be curbed. It sweeps him over the edge of the second act of *Siegfried* into the third, and over Wagner's relinquishment of the work that left it suspended here some twelve years. 'Yes, I arose / and went on my way, / till I came to that fiery peak' (he now obliterates altogether the episode with the Wanderer and his spear); 'I passed through those dangers, / I found the maid . . . / sleeping . . . my glorious bride!' The excitement of the ascent, the long pages of utter stillness at the mountain-top, his bafflement, his fear at last, seeing a woman for the first time, his efforts to wake her, the fearful kiss with which he did so, and its eventual outcome — all this is compressed into three pages.

His conclusion ('Oh, then like burning fire / I was held by lovely Brünnhilde's arms!') takes us to the end of *Siegfried*, the consummation of the lovers' long and tortuous courtship, but leaves us musically poised upon the cadence that ends their duet just after Brünnhilde's awakening. Here the present intrudes for the second time. The first reminiscence from *Twilight* itself had been intimate, known only to Siegfried and played only by four clarinets; the second is public, violent, horrible. The cadence hangs in the air; Gunther springs up in horror; the harsh Hagen dissonance (hideously scored — 8 stopped horns, low oboes, english horn, clarinets, a stab of four trombones, a blanket of strings) slithers up in parallel as the watchful ravens, knowing the moment, circle over Siegfried and fly off towards the river. He turns to follow their flight; Hagen, even here cracking a black joke ('and can you tell / what those ravens have said?') thrusts his spear into his exposed back; and night begins to fall. The curse, silent since the end of the Rhinemaiden scene, is thrust harshly up against Hagen the manhunter. Siegfried swings his shield high as if to crush his shadow-brother; but his strength fails, and his motif ends on a dissonance, the same that crowned his ascent through the flames disguised as Gunther [23]. That had collapsed onto the Tarnhelm-motif, by which the disguise was done; now there is no more deception, it is 'Siegfried, no other' who is felled, and his motif falls onto the rhythm that will dominate his funeral music [89], heard here four times as its anticipatory upbeat. Hagen turns calmly away and walks off through the twilight, having answered the vassals' appalled question with a snatch of the blood-brotherhood oath ('falsehood is punished'). The 'fate' motif [38] sounds twice, separated by funeral-rhythm drum-taps, prophesying a passage still further ahead, in Brünnhilde's final scene. The sympathetic vassals and grief-stricken Gunther gather round to support the dying man. The intrusion of present horrors into rapt reliving of the past has lasted only 32 bars. Now Act Three of *Siegfried* resumes.

The rate of recapitulation has become steadily slower — one-and-a-half acts in two pages — the next events (bridging the *Tristan-Meistersinger* expedition) in three, slowing always towards the original broadness. After the 32 bars of violent action and shocked reaction, it broadens still further. Siegfried, continuing his tales of boyhood even as he expires, goes back to the most wonderful of all his adventures. As he '*opens his eyes radiantly*', the music returns exactly to Brünnhilde's awakening gestures when *her* eyes were opened. Only the words are different, painfully intermittent as he struggles to hold the vision. The shortened repeat as she greeted sun, light, day, is not needed; thereafter the recall of the music is again total. At first the words are poignantly different: Brünnhilde's 'Long was my sleep; / but now I wake: / Who is the man / wakes me to life?' becomes Siegfried's 'Who has forced you / back to your sleep? / Who bound you in slumber again?' One crotchet's-worth of major triad not in *Siegfried* illuminates the pathos of his questions. In the next section, still musically identical, he dislocates his own former words: in life he had answered her question thus — 'I have braved the dangers / blazing round your rock; / from your head I unclasped the helm; / Siegfried wakes you, / brings you to life.' In dying this becomes: 'Your bridegroom came, / to kiss you awake; / he frees you, again, / breaking your fetters. / He lives in Brünnhilde's love!' The third section, however, begins to elide as his strength ebbs. The section begins identically, but whereas Brünnhilde, hailing gods, world, Erda, rose to a climax of glory, Siegfried gutters out, with [59] declining all the way, and a more and more exquisitely tender version of [58] (whose first appearance was as bright and fierce as the light they had welcomed together). 'Ah! See those eyes, / open for ever!' Though what has gone wrong and why he is struck down is never untangled for him, as he dies he too sees clearly; his deception, duplicity, treachery, are washed away by the music. Siegfried's death (again we recall the emphasis of Wagner's first title) links two turning-points in the tetralogy: its hero's greatest moment when he wakens Brünnhilde, and his lowest when he has betrayed her and she has brought about his killing; they are united in the farthest-flung arc of memory-architecture ever achieved in music. Between them comes almost the entire action of *Twilight*, and only as the great span reaches its farthest extent do we see clearly why the work opens with the fusion of Brünnhilde's awakening, Siegfried's death, and the waters of the Rhine. The tetralogy's highest and lowest points are united here with what began *The Rhinegold* and what will end everything: the waters of the river, enclosing their gold, purged of its curse. Wagner's two titles fuse; *Siegfried's Death* intermeshes with the *Twilight of the Gods*.

The funeral music is recapitulation of a different kind, working together many related motifs into a self-contained structure, a threnody in C minor marking the hero's passing, recalling his ancestry, celebrating him in both tonic and relative major, all hung upon the rhythm first heard just after he was toppled. Its early stages set out Siegfried's family-tree. This necessarily returns to the part of *The Valkyrie* not yet revisited in *Twilight*, ie Act One. First comes the Volsungs' theme [33]; during its second strain the moon illuminates the receding funeral procession, perhaps recalling the Volsungs' only moment of happiness; then comes the theme of their destiny [31] and the

35

Jean Cox as Siegfried in the Götz Friedrich production at Covent Garden, 1976 (photo: Donald Southern)

love-music of Siegmund and Sieglinde [30], then a huge build-up to the apotheosis of their son, the Volsungs' noblest scion. All these themes are presented in diatonic splendour: his sword, in the C major inseparable from it since Notung first shone gently for Siegmund [27]; his own theme [39]; then the grandiose elevation of his horn-call, confirming E♭ as his heroic resting-place, and forged into the rhythm of the tattoo which has also made the gigantic chordal flourishes separating his three themes. Tovey deplored this transformation as bombastic and forced; but it is, appropriately, the boldest instance of an attribute becoming a person. The very crudeness of the transformation makes the contrast more telling as, in the subtle transition which follows, Siegfried's horn-call again represents the living man in Gutrune's frightened imagination, while the procession returns with his corpse.

This change of scene is punctuated by the curse, in close conjunction with Hagen's version of the Rhinegold-call. Our dazed attention is drawn to *things* again; the gold and its curse still lie on Siegfried's finger. We hear the curse only three times more. The first is almost immediate; Gunther and Hagen squabble over possession of the ring (recalling Fasolt and Fafner, Mime and Alberich); Gunther is killed, Hagen claims his own from the dead hand but the whole arm rises threateningly, and at this moment Brünnhilde, absent from all this pettiness, comes forward to take control. She has been in communion with the Rhine and its maidens: they have reached her as they said they would, and completed the information Waltraute gave her when telling her what to do with the ring.

Her final scene is the most important and elaborate area of developing recapitulation in *Twilight*; to untwist every strand and relate it to its origins would involve revisiting most of the tetralogy. Everything she knows is here; what she does not, we have heard again from those who do. In the spacious opening paragraph, introduced with fate-motif and drum-beats from the silence after Siegfried's death-blow (which recall the solemn portents when she appeared to announce Siegmund's death), she calls upon the vassals to raise a pyre upon which she will also die. That this music grows directly out of the Norns' scene in the prologue and Waltraute's narration in Act One, makes a purposeful identification of the two final fires, here and at Valhalla. Lofty command yields to intimacy as she contemplates Siegfried's body and puts the paradox of the truest friend and lover who yet broke oaths and betrayed his love as never before. The third stage resolves the paradox; to music taken directly from Erda's denunciation of Wotan's falsehood in the last act of *Siegfried*, she tells him, through the attendant ravens, that she now understands clearly how it came to be, how it had to be so; and to music taken directly from her scene with Waltraute (with one sublime addition) she dispatches the ravens with the god's repose vouchsafed him at last.

The curse has been heard here for the second time since Siegfried's death, but its power is nearly gone. Just for a little longer she holds the accursed object, drawing the ring off the dead man's finger and reflecting on what it has done — (*lit.*) 'I claim my inheritance — accursed ring — I grasp your gold, and cast you away' — word and deed for which the whole work has waited. Only once has anyone wanted other than to keep it, and the other times it has been yielded are both recalled here: Wotan, with intense reluctance and only when compelled by a *dea ex machina*; and Siegfried himself, who gave it willingly to Brünnhilde with an ardour conspicuously unmarked by the curse-motif, but who then couldn't part with it quite so easily to the Rhinemaidens, in that crucial scene which makes a clear parallel with what Brünnhilde does now. As she dons it again, it is clean. She is not a victim of the curse; her action is voluntary, for the benefit of all as well as herself. The fire will consume her lover's dead and her living body; from its ashes the river-daughters will claim their own and guard it better. She knows that when she ignites the pyre, Loge will start the bigger blaze that marks the end of the gods. The ravens have stayed to see the first brand cast, before flying off to the Valkyrie rock to summon Loge for the congenial task of razing Valhalla. They thus miss Brünnhilde's final ecstasy, the reunion with Siegfried in a consummatory blaze of his theme, her Valkyrie-music and the motif of 'redemption by love' [40].

The curse is active to the end for those who think in its terms. Cupidity still drives Hagen. As the Rhine rises to receive its gold, the curse and Rhinegold-call fuse for a final embrace as he lunges wildly after the Rhinemaidens and is dragged to his death, shadow following substance to the last. The maddened waters, having extinguished the earthly fire, return to their bed, and the girls are seen playing with their trinket. The gold and the curse have counter-pointed each other throughout *Twilight* because their meaning is intertwined; the waters have been ravished of their treasure which thereby becomes unclean; its restoration to them cleanses it and restores what is right. But this apparently simple act involves a complex tangle, every thread of which has to be sorted out. As part of this an old order has to disappear, and now comes the second fire, promised by the Norns, rehearsed by Waltraute, implicit in Loge's final words in *Rhinegold* — the destruction of Valhalla. Its music is intercut with lilting strains of primordial river-music, and the apotheosis of love and

Brünnhilde's immolation scene at the end of the 1979 Bayreuth 'Ring', produced by Patrice Chéreau, designed by Richard Peduzzi, with costumes by Jacques Schmidt: Gwyneth Jones as Brünnhilde. (photo: Festspielleitung Bayreuth)

womanhood swells warmly above. Just before the flames seize upon the gods themselves, Siegfried's theme rises up for the last time; then as flames obscure them, their end, *the* end, the twilight of the gods itself [25] makes a vast neapolitan cadence onto all that remains — the eternal feminine in the skies, the clear golden river beneath, and, perhaps, Alberich in its depths awaiting for ever his next opportunity.

The Questionable Lightness of Being: Brünnhilde's Peroration to 'The Ring'

Christopher Wintle

The musical correlative of a dramatic ending is a perfect cadence. Yet when we listen for a definitive cadence in the home key of D♭ major at the end of *The Ring*, we encounter a paradox: there are two such cadences. Both occur during the course of Brünnhilde's concluding monologue, and together they celebrate the conclusion of the two interlocked narratives that comprise the cycle: the tragedy of Wotan on the one hand, and the Siegfried 'fairy-tale' (as Carl Dahlhaus has called it) on the other:

Example 1

This first cadence is tenebral, grave and crepuscular: the motion draws towards, and eventually achieves the repose that Brünnhilde invokes for the head of the gods with its pair of concluding held notes marked *sehr langsam* (very slow): the utterance is characterized by a restraint (*pp*) appropriate not only to a child's final benediction of its parent, but also to our foreknowledge of the combustion that awaits Valhalla (it will blaze to the neapolitan harmony marked*): and the funeral brass instrumentation is epitomized by the wan sonority of the bass trumpet, that plays the cadence-figure (x) from the Valhalla music. On the other hand, the second cadence —

Example 2

— is jubilant, impetuous, luminous and replete with aspiration: the motion intensifies, the string lines soar, the dynamics swell to *ff* (immediately after, they burst into a series of *forzandi*), and Brünnhilde's words are snatched, syncopated, and set in the radiant upper register of her vocal range. Both cadences complete a descending linear progression from A♭ to D♭, as the examples show, and both are followed by actions: the first by the preparation of Siegfried's (and by extension Wotan's) funeral pyre, and the second by Brünnhilde's leap into the flames on the back of her steed Grane. But beyond this, the contrasts are so great as to seem reciprocal; and if we think of the second cadence as a *transformation* of the first, we may begin to understand the significance of *The Ring*'s peroration.

Let us look more closely at Example 1.

There is an irony to this passage, which emerges only when its musical and dramatic functions are considered in tandem. Formally, it recapitulates Waltraute's earlier entreaty to Brünnhilde to return the ring to its owners. She relays Wotan's words, whispered 'as if in a dream', from Valhalla: 'if she [Brünnhilde] returned the ring to the daughters of the deep Rhine, God and the World would be redeemed from the burden of [Alberich's] curse.'[1] At this point, of course, nothing is further from Brünnhilde's mind: to restore the ring would be to cede her most cherished token of Siegfried's love. And in any case, she has already acquired too much wisdom not to recognise Valhalla for what it is: an emblem of Wotan's worldly authority, to be sure, but also the kitsch, chauvinist paradise that has already been rejected contemptuously by the ill-fated Siegmund, and from which, indeed, she has been harshly and irrevocably expelled. There is more, however, to this emblem than mere pomp, as the Valhalla theme [8] itself reveals. At its conclusion, the rocking motif and the subsequent cadential figure together depict its regressive nature: the gods are cradled 'safe from fear and dread' (*wiegen* is the word Alberich uses), and their portals are closed (cadentially) against the threatening outer world of 'dark elves'. And it is this false domestic and psychological security that Waltraute is also seeking to shore up. Her entreaty, though, is significantly incomplete:

Example 3

WALTRAUTE

The rocking motif (y) freezes into a *ppp* chord, and the subsequent, comforting cadence figure is disconcertingly absent. Eventually, in her concluding monologue, Brünnhilde complies with Waltraute's entreaty: yet the context has changed utterly. 'All is now clear' to her. The falseness of Valhalla is irredeemable. Her words purge the world of the illusions harboured by the gods. The rocking motif ((y) in Example 1) now lulls Wotan to the eternal rest he once dreaded, a rest she seals with the finality of the cadence figure (x).

In fact, this cadence figure has had a fascinating and illuminating history

[1] For the sake of detailed discussion, most of the translations from the German here are literal ones.

*The scornful laughter of the Nibelung: Alberich (Derek Hammond-Stroud) jeers at Mime
(Gregory Dempsey) in 'Siegfried', ENO, 1973 (photo: Anthony Crickmay)*

during the course of the cycle. But before tracing it, we must look more closely
at Example 2.

The cadence here shows Brünnhilde's concluding action restoring her to
her former self: the anticipated D♭ major harmony beneath the word *Weib* is
replaced by the Valkyrean augmented harmony C#/F/A. A little earlier in the
monologue, she has turned to her steed: 'Are you enticed', she asks
confidingly, 'by the laughing flame?' The question is so bizarre as to have
drawn a caustic comment from Theodor Adorno: 'in the teeth of the cult of
the prevention of cruelty to animals,' he declared, 'she even insists that her
horse should neigh with joy as it leaps into the flames.' The comment,
however, should not deflect our attention from the importance of the keyword
here, *laughing*. Brünnhilde's joy is far from that of a willing accomplice to an
ostentatious act of Indian self-sacrifice (*sati*), as Adorno claimed. In fact it
marks the culmination of another process of transformation and purgation
that also extends through *The Ring*. Laughter abounds in the cycle, and is of
essentially three kinds. The first is entirely literal, and reveals all that is
craven, malevolent and avaricious in the male psyche. It includes Mime's
pathetic tittering (*kichernd*) as he unwittingly informs Siegfried of his
treacherous designs upon his life; Alberich's jeering to the forging motif [17]
at Mime's death (*hohnlachend*); and the strident *Schadenfreude* of Hagen

(*grell lachend*) as he hears the story of Mime's demise from the lips of the fated Siegfried. Fricka, too, complains to Wotan that it is his 'laughing lightness' that has brought the gods into disrepute. Then, by contrast, there is an entirely metaphorical laughter, which is born of the eternally feminine nature of Brünnhilde, herself representative of Wotan's 'laughing joy'. This finds its fullest expression in the concluding love-duet of *Siegfried*: 'laughing must I love you', sings Brünnhilde, 'laughing will I lose my sight, laughing shall I go into the ground.' In *The Valkyrie*, moreover, Wotan has even asked Fricka to rejoice (*lachend der Liebe*) in the pure, incestuous love of Siegmund for Sieglinde. There can be no more tangible affirmation of her death-defying love, therefore, than this leap of Brünnhilde into the flames.

The third, and most interesting, kind of laughter, however, is the untutored, natural and purely callow mirth of Siegfried. It functions narratively as an agent of truth and, in one central instance, mediates between the concerns of the two cadences. We encounter it at Siegfried's first appearance, where his rollicking guffaws to his own theme [45] establish the deviousness of his guardian Mime, who is being pursued around their cave by the bear Siegfried has brought in from the forest; his first mocking response to Fafner indicts the length to which the giant has been driven in his determination to guard the gold; and Siegfried's description of his reforged sword's participation in the laughter (*nun lacht ihm sein heller Schein*) suggests an important image of rebirth. Most strikingly, the confrontation between Wotan and Siegfried (in *Siegfried*, Act Three) provokes laughter on both sides that is mutually incomprehensible. At first, Wotan, cannily disguised as the Wanderer, takes pleasure in his surrogate son (in fact, his grandson). He breaks into a contented laugh. The entirely naive Siegfried takes offence. Why should he be mocked by such an old man, he asks. Wotan advises him to hold his tongue, and hints at their blood-relationship: one of Siegfried's eyes, he remarks, makes up for his own missing one. The music reinforces Wotan's warning here, by deploying the power of the Valhalla theme, which proceeds to its affirmative cadential figure (x):

Example 4

from (8)

43

But all this is too much for Siegfried, who refuses to allow the cadence to complete its course (the bass in Example 4 remains on the dominant), and disrupts its flow with his callow laughter. Siegfried here points to the illusory nature of Wotan's power, which he shortly confirms by breaking the god's spear with his own sword (ironically, a gift to his father Siegmund from Wotan himself). Later, of course, the rawness of his humour will be tamed by the love of Brünnhilde. That it has already effected a transformation in the drama may be seen by comparing these events with those that conclude *The Rhinegold*:

Example 5

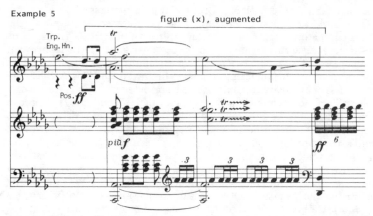

There, through the falsest laughter in the cycle, the assembled gods had mocked the Rhine-daughters for the loss of their gold, by combining the falsely affirmative cadential figure (x) of the Valhalla music, with the laughing figuration of the Firegod who will eventually destroy them all (Example 5).

Here, then, is one of the ways in which the close that marks the end of the era of Valhalla (Example 1) is related to that which looks forward to a new world of love, lightness, and a purified laughter (Example 2). There are, however, other, less obvious links between these closes that puts this transformation into a critical perspective.

Brünnhilde's greeting to her dead husband Siegfried (Example 2) is accompanied by two motifs: the one associated with Siegfried himself [39], and that first introduced in *The Valkyrie*, at the point where Brünnhilde reveals to Sieglinde that she bears 'the world's greatest hero' in her womb [40]. The words accompanying the second of these motifs [40] in its original context reflect the passion of Sieglinde's response: 'O most sublime wonder', she sings, thanking Brünnhilde the 'glorious maid', for bringing 'comfort': 'May the recompense of my thanks laugh for you some day' (*'meines Dankes Lohn lache die einst'*). The music is set, broadly speaking, in G major. But when, at the end of *Twilight of the Gods*, these sentiments and motifs are recalled in Example 2, the harmonic context, although moving towards the tonic Db major, is nevertheless fluid. It is notable, however, that the motif celebrating the 'sublime wonder' [40] is set around the note Eb. Of course, this note and its tonality recall the unbroken harmoniousness of the opening of *The Rhinegold*, as well as, relatedly, the supreme, integrated love-duet between Brünnhilde and Siegfried from the Prologue of *Twilight of the Gods*. This nostalgia also embraces, importantly, the Eb major in which the first

44

Norn describes the woodland paradise, the terrestrial equivalent to the original state of Nature, where the World Ash-Tree once flourished.

Example 6

The beginning and end of the first part of the Norn's description is shown in Example 6, which sees a modulation from E♭ to its dominant. There are two remarkable features about this passage: first, all the motifs are familiar, and secondly, this paradise is at once described nostalgically as something irretrievably lost. Bar 1 establishes the connection with the Rhine music [1] from the opening of the cycle; bar 3, on the other hand, establishes the narrative position of the Norn, conscious that the two awakening chords in the orchestra [57] are cast in the dreadful, portentous key of E♭ minor, sounding the same stark tonic harmony with which Hagen will justify the slaughter of Siegfried as 'the holiest right of the hunter'. The Norn's vocal line, moreover, adopts the 'circular' contour of the motif associated with the ring itself [6]. Especially revealing is the music at bars 8 and 9, which follows the description of the woodland as it once was: astonishingly, the closing formula is that of the Valhalla music, figure (x). This is not fortuitous. Six bars later, this figure is repeated, and is at once followed by the description of Wotan's appearance in the wood, his sacrifice of an eye in exchange for drinking at wisdom's well, and his fatally destructive breaking of the branch from the Ash-Tree to form his spear. The implication of the correspondence is clear: Valhalla, which Wotan conceives the moment he drinks, attempts to recreate the security of this woodland paradise by harnessing its (cadential) symbol of stability. When Brünnhilde, therefore, at the end of *Twilight of the Gods*, closes the Valhalla music (Example 1), she does not merely purge figure (x) of its false security, but restores it to its 'original' state of nature.

How, then, do these detailed observations illumine our understanding of *The Ring* as a whole? In fact, two possible interpretations may be drawn from the analysis, both of which need to be recognised if the measure of the work is to be gained adequately.

The first asks us to accept the simple transformation that we perceive in the opera house. This is not only epitomized by the move from the cadence of Example 1 to that of Example 2, but is also summed up in the last minute or so of music: Valhalla has fallen before the new order ushered in by Siegfried, the gods burn in the heavens, and we are left to contemplate Brünnhilde's uplifting self-sacrifice. Significantly, the tonic key in which we end, D♭ major, which was associated with the corporeal Valhalla in *The Rhinegold*, is now articulated by the theme of the incorporeal 'sublime wonder' celebrated by Brünnhilde. At first encounter, it is hard not to see a Biblical model standing behind this transformation, with Wotan's Old Testament 'letter of the law' ceding to Brünnhilde's New Testament 'spirit of love'. Interestingly, though, the Old Testament parallels are the more striking: most of the protagonists (above all Wotan) are guiltily preoccupied with the need to regain their lost Eden; the burdens incurred by this loss (in Wagner, of the gold from the Rhine) are passed through the generations; and everyone lives under the shadow of a prophetic determinism that is as inexorable as it is Apocalyptic. (One may compare Erda's: 'all of the past I know: all things that are, all things that shall be — all I know . . . all things that are, perish', with Isaiah 37: 'have you not heard that I determined it long ago, I planned from days of old what I now bring to pass, that you should make fortified cities crash into heaps of ruins, while their inhabitants, shorn of strength are dismayed and confounded?') From a New Testament point of view, however, it is harder to think of Siegfried as the Redeemer of man: not only is his love consummately sexual, but unlike Brünnhilde, he is not prey to genuinely human sufferings and temptations (erotic fear notwithstanding). Moreover, Brünnhilde's 'redeeming' acts of restoration and self-sacrifice are feminine ones, for all that they celebrate the harmony of man-and-woman.

The second interpretation, which arises out of reflection upon the

Brünnhilde's joy: Rita Hunter at ENO (photo: Reg Wilson).

ramifications of Examples 1 and 2, appears to contradict the first. The history of figure (x) has taught us that Valhalla represents, in part, an attempt to retrieve a lost paradise, which is associated with the key of E♭ major. This effort at reparation on Wotan's part, however, has been laughingly brushed aside by Siegfried, who later regains this paradise for himself by celebrating his consummate love for Brünnhilde in E♭ major once more. Yet, despite the efforts of the narrative to persuade us otherwise, we can understand neither Siegfried (Wotan's blood-relation) nor Brünnhilde (his 'eternal side') as entirely free agents: they are as much an extension of Wotan's all-too-human eugenic fantasy as they are of his loins. So it comes as no surprise that their love turns out to be as doomed as the World Ash-Tree itself. In this world, it appears impossible to sustain E♭ major for very long (and, significantly, Wagner deliberately chose not the end the cycle in this key). As audience, therefore, the best we can do, it seems on reflection, is to purge ourselves, as Brünnhilde purged Wotan, of the worldly illusions attendant upon our own D♭ major existence, inspired by an *idea* of paradise that, as Brünnhilde demonstrates, can at best only lead to a 'laughing death' and a denial of ordinary human life. From this point of view, the deaths of Siegfried, Brünnhilde and Wotan in the last act of *Twilight of the Gods* serve only to confirm the pessimism and renunciation that Wotan increasingly embraces during the course of *The Ring*.

Neither interpretation, of course, stands happily on its own. To the extent that Ludwig Feuerbach maintained, in the *Essence of Christianity* (which Wagner read, according to Ernest Newman, around 1850), that 'every advance in religion is a deeper self-knowledge', and that religion itself is no more than 'the dream of the human mind', the profundity of Wagner's humane, atheistic portrayal of the god Wotan must make *The Ring* count as one of the most important nineteenth-century contributions to the anthropology that Feuerbach insisted that theology must become. Hence, the second interpretation must hold good. But Wagner's mythic dreams may still testify to the quasi-religious, redemptive, Apocalyptic aspirations of a suffering humanity; and it is these aspirations that are fulfilled by the story of Siegfried and Brünnhilde. The first interpretation, therefore, must also hold good. But the psychological dependence that this argument suggests of the dreams and aspirations upon the gloomy broodings of Wotan is not this clear-cut. We empathize equally with Wotan and Brünnhilde. Thus by offering us the fantasy and the tragedy together, and by asking us to respond to, and reflect upon both equivalently, Wagner created in *The Ring* a work of quite extraordinary ambiguity. And this, perhaps, is what the two cadences with which we began, together with all their ramifications, eventually signify.

Thematic Guide

devised by
Lionel Friend

Each Opera Guide to a part of *The Ring* refers to one general list of leitmotifs in which the themes are numbered according to their first appearance in the cycle. The complete list is given here.

51

[21]

[22]

[23]

[24] cf. [1b]

[25]

[26]

[27]   a   b   c

[28]

[29]

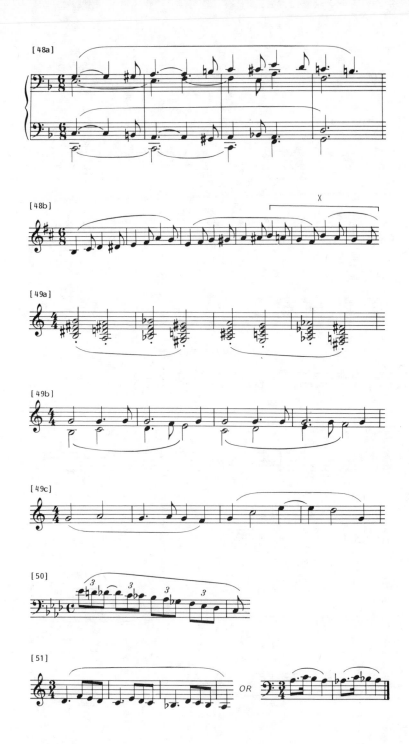

57

Blut - brüd-er-schaft

Katherine Pring as Waltraute at ENO, 1976 (photo: John Garner)

An illustration from 'The Illustrated London News', December 26, 1903 of the production at Covent Garden earlier that year (Royal Opera House Archives)

Twilight of the Gods
Götterdämmerung

Third Day of the Festival Play
'The Ring of the Nibelung'

Music-Drama in a Prologue and Three Acts
by Richard Wagner

Poem by Richard Wagner
English translation by Andrew Porter

Götterdämmerung was first performed at the Festspielhaus, Bayreuth on August 17, 1876. The first performance in England was at Her Majesty's Theatre, London in 1882. The first performance in the United States was at the Metropolitan Opera House, New York on January 25, 1888.

This translation was commissioned by English National Opera (then Sadler's Wells Opera) and first performed at the London Coliseum on January 29, 1971. The full cycle was first given in July and August 1973 and the opera was recorded in full performance at the London Coliseum in December 1975 by EMI.

The German text for the whole cycle was first published in 1853. Archaisms of spelling and an excess of punctuation have been removed but the original verse layout has been retained.

The stage directions are literal translations of those written by Wagner and do not reflect any actual production. The numbers in square brackets refer to the Thematic Guide.

CHARACTERS

Siegfried	*tenor*
Gunther	*bass-baritone*
Hagen	*bass*
Alberich	*bass-baritone*
Brünnhilde	*soprano*
Gutrune	*soprano*
Waltraute	*mezzo-soprano*
The three Norns	*contralto, mezzo-soprano and soprano*
The three Rhinemaidens	*soprano, mezzo-soprano and contralto*
Chorus of Vassals and Women	

The three Norns in the Prelude of the ENO production, 1976 with (left to right) Elizabeth Connell, Anne Evans and Anne Collins (photo: Reg Wilson)

Prelude

On the Valkyrie Rock. The scene is the same as at the close of 'The Valkyrie'. It is night. Firelight shines up from the depths of the background.

The three Norns, tall female figures in long, dark veil-like drapery. The First (the oldest) is lying in the foreground on the right, under the spreading pine-tree; the Second (younger) reclines on a rock in front of the cave; the Third (the youngest) sits in the centre at back on a rock below the peak. Gloomy silence and stillness. [57, 1c, 24, 38, 62]

FIRST NORN
(without moving) [24]

What light shines down there?   Welch Licht leuchtet dort?

SECOND NORN

Can it be day so soon?   Dämmert der Tag schon auf?

THIRD NORN

Loge's flames   [14] Loges Heer
leap and flicker round the rock.   lodert feurig um den Fels.
It is night.   [62] Noch ist's Nacht.
And so we should sing as we spin.   Was spinnen und singen wir nicht?

SECOND NORN
(to the First)

Let us be spinning and singing;   Wollen wir spinnen und singen,
but where, where tie the cord?   woran spannst du das Seil?

FIRST NORN
(rises, unwinds a golden rope from herself, and ties one end of it to a branch of the pine-tree.)

Though good or ill may come,   So gut und schlimm es geh',
weaving the cord, I'll sing now.   [1b] schling ich das Seil und singe.
At the World Ash-tree   [63] An der Weltesche
once I wove,   wob ich einst,
when fair and green   da gross und stark
there grew from its branches   dem Stamm entgrünte
verdant and shady leaves.   weihlicher Äste Wald.
Those cooling shadows   [8e] Im kühlen Schatten
sheltered a spring;   rauscht' ein Quell,
wisdom's voice   [63] Weisheit raunend
I heard in its waves;   rann sein Gewell';
I sang my holy song.   [8e] da sang ich heil'gen Sinn.

A valiant god   [27c] Ein kühner Gott
came to drink at the spring;   trat zum Trunk an den Quell;
and the price he had to pay   8a,b] seiner Augen eines
was the loss of an eye.   zahlt' er als ewigen Zoll.
From the World Ash-tree   Von der Weltesche
mighty Wotan broke a branch;   brach da Wotan einen Ast;
and his spear was shaped   [9a] eines Speeres Schaft
from that branch he tore from the tree.   [27a]entschnitt der Starke dem Stamm.

As year succeeded year,   In langer Zeiten lauf
the wound slowly weakened the tree;   zehrte die Wunde den Wald;
dry, leafless, and barren,   [1b, 25] falb fielen die Blätter,
death seized on the tree;   dürr darbte der Baum,
whispering waters   traurig versiegte
then failed in the spring: des Quelles Trank:
grief and sorrow   trüben Sinnes
stole through my song.   [63] ward mein Gesang.
And so I weave   Doch, web' ich heut
at the World Ash-tree no more;   an der Weltesche nicht mehr,

65

today I use these branches
to fasten the cord.
Sing, my sister;
take up the thread:
say what happened then.

[62] muss mir die Tanne
taugen zu fesseln das Seil:
singe, Schwester,
dir werf ich's zu.
[37] Weisst du, wie das wird?

SECOND NORN

(winds the rope that has been thrown to her round a projecting rock at the entrance of the cave.)

Wotan made
holy laws and treaties;
then Wotan
cut their words in the spear:
he held it to rule all the world,
until the day
a hero broke it in two;
with shining sword
he destroyed the god's holy laws.
Then Wotan ordered
Walhall's heroes
to hack down
the World Ash's trunk,
and to cut its branches to pieces.
The Ash-tree fell;
dry were the waters of the spring!
And so today
I must tie our cord to the rock.
Sing, my sister;
take up the thread.
What will happen now?

Treu beratner
Verträge Runen
schnitt Wotan
[60] in des Speeres Schaft;
[9a] den hielt er als Haft der Welt.
Ein kühner Held
zerhieb im Kampfe den Speer;
in Trümmer sprang
der Verträge heiliger Haft.
[8a] Da hiess Wotan
Walhalls Helden
der Weltesche
[25] welkes Geäst
mit dem Stamm in Stücke zu fällen.
Die Esche sank,
[63] ewig versiegte der Quell!
[62] Fessle ich heut
an den scharfen Fels das Seil:
singe, Schwester,
dir werf ich's zu.
[37] Weisst du, wie das wird?

THIRD NORN

(catching the rope and throwing the end behind her.)

That mighty hall
the giants have raised —
there the immortals and heroes
all have assembled;
there sits Wotan on high.
But all around it
there are heaped
like a wall
huge, mighty branches:
the World Ash-tree once they were!
When that wood
blazes furious and bright,
when the flames
seize on that glorious abode,
the rule of the gods is ended;
darkness falls on the gods.
What happens then?
Oh take up the cord and the song;
from the north
I now must throw it to you.
Spin, my sister, and sing on!

Es ragt die Burg,
von Riesen gebaut:
mit der Götter und Helden
heiliger Sippe
[25] sitzt dort Wotan im Saal.
[60] Gehau'ner Scheite
hohe Schicht
ragt zuhauf
rings um die Halle:
[63] die Weltesche war dies einst!
Brennt das Holz
heilig brünstig und hell,
sengt die Glut
sehrend den glänzenden Saal:
[9a, 8a] der ewigen Götter Ende
[25] dämmert ewig da auf.
[38] Wisset ihr noch?
[62] So windet von neuem das Seil;
von Norden wieder
werf ich's dir nach.
Spinne, Schwester, und singe!

*She throws the rope to the Second Norn. The Second Norn casts it to the First, who loosens the
rope from the branch and fastens it to another.*

FIRST NORN

(looking toward the back)

Is that the day
or the flickering firelight?
For sadness dims my eyes;
I see no longer
those sacred visions
which Loge once

[13a] Dämmert der Tag?
Oder leuchtet die Lohe?
Getrübt trügt sich mein Blick;
nicht hell eracht ich
das heilig Alte,
da Loge einst

would light up in radiant fire.
Tell me, what was his fate?

entbrannte in lichter Gluth.
[37] Weisst du, was aus ihm ward?

SECOND NORN
(once again winding the rope that has been thrown to her around the rock)

By the spear's enchantment
Wotan enslaved him;
Loge counselled the god.
But he longed for freedom,
  tried to escape him,
broke the laws on the spear.
Then, once again
by the spear he was summoned;
  ordered by Wotan,
Brünnhilde's rock he surrounded.
Know you what happens now?

[9a] Durch des Speeres Zauber
[13a] zähmte ihn Wotan;
Räte raunt' er dem Gott.
An des Schaftes Runen,
  frei sich zu raten,
nagte zehrend sein Zahn:
[9a] Da, mit des Speeres
zwingender Spitze
  bannte ihn Wotan,
[13a]Brünnhildes Fels zu umbrennen.
[37] Weisst du, was aus ihm wird?

THIRD NORN
(again throwing behind her the end of the rope as it comes to her)

Now the god will seize
the spear that was shattered,
  drive it deep
in the breast of the fiery god:
then, when the flames
  leap from the spear,
those flames he'll cast
at the World Ash-tree
whose branches are heaped around Walhall.

[60] Des zerschlagnen Speeres
stechende Splitter
  taucht' einst Wotan
dem Brünstigen tief in die Brust:
zehrender Brand
  zündet da auf;
den wirft der Gott
[63] in der Weltesche
[8] zuhauf geschichtete Scheite.

She throws the rope back; the Second Norn coils it and throws it back to the First.
[42]

SECOND NORN

Let us discover
when that will be.
Spin, then, sisters, our cord!

Wollt ihr wissen,
[38] wie das wird?
Schwinget, Schwestern, das Seil!

FIRST NORN
(fastening the rope again)

The night fades;
dark are my senses:
these feeble threads
have slipped from my grasp;
the rope is tangled and frayed.
A hideous sight
wounds me, clouding my eyes:
  the Rhinegold
which Alberich stole —
say, what became of him?

[42] Die Nacht weicht;
nichts mehr gewahr ich:
des Seiles Fäden
find ich nicht mehr;
verflochten ist das Geflecht.
[6] Ein wüstes Gesicht
[25] wirrt mir wütend den Sinn.
[3, 4x] Das Rheingold
raubte Alberich einst.
[38] Weisst du, was aus ihm ward?

SECOND NORN
(with anxious haste winding the rope around the jagged rock at the mouth of the cave)

The threads are breaking,
  cut by the crag;
the rope loses
  its hold on the rock;
it hangs ravelled and torn;
  while need and greed
rise from the Nibelung's ring:
  and Alberich's curse
tears at the strands of the cord.
Ah, what will happen next?

[6] Der Steines Schärfe
Schnitt in das Seil;
  nicht fest spannt mehr
der Fäden Gespinst;
verwirrt ist das Geweb'.
[62] Aus Not und Neid
ragt mir des Niblungen Ring:
[5] ein rächender Fluch
nagt meiner Fäden Geflecht.
[27] Weisst du, was daraus wird?

THIRD NORN
(hastily catching the rope thrown to her)

The rope is too slack;

Zu locker das Seil,

67

it reaches not.
If I must cast it   [45]
back to the north,
the sagging rope must be stretched.

(She tugs at the rope, which breaks in the middle.) [23]

It splits!

SECOND NORN

It splits!

FIRST NORN

It splits!

The three Norns start up in terror, and gather at the centre of the stage; they grasp the piec⟨
of the broken rope and bind their bodies together with them.

THE THREE NORNS

An end now to our wisdom!   [25]
The world hears   [23]
our counsel no more!

THIRD NORN

Away!   [42]

SECOND NORN

To Erda!

FIRST NORN

Away!

They vanish. [38] *Dawn. The red glow of sunrise grows; the firelight from below grows fainter*
Sunrise. Broad daylight. Siegfried and Brünnhilde enter from the cave; he is fully armed; she
leads her horse by the bridle. [64, 30a, 65, 34]

BRÜNNHILDE

To deeds of glory,   [65]
brave beloved!
My love for you
bids you be gone.
One care constrains me,
makes me linger:
I've not repaid you   [66]
for all you brought.

What gods have given me,
I've given you:
all that they taught me,
now is yours;
all of this maiden's
wisdom and strength
given to the man   [59]
who is now my master.

I'm wise no more,   [65]
though my heart is full:
in love I'm rich,
though emptied of power,
I fear that you
may now despise me;
how can I serve you?
I've no more to give!   [66]

SIEGFRIED

More you have given to me [64]
than I can rightly grasp.   [66]
Forgive me if your lessons [65]
have left me still untaught.

mir langt es nicht.
Soll ich nach Norden
neigen das Ende,
straffer sei es gestreckt!

Es riss!

Es riss!

Es riss!

Zu End' ewiges Wissen!
Der Welt melden
Weise nichts mehr.

Hinab!

Zur Mutter!

Hinab!

Zu neuen Taten,
teurer Helde,
wie liebt' ich dich,
liess ich dich nicht?
Ein einzig' Sorgen
lässt mich säumen:
dass dir zu wenig
mein Wert gewann!

Was Götter mich wiesen,
gab ich dir:
heiliger Runen
reichen Hort;
doch meiner Stärke
magdlichen Stamm
nahm mir der Held,
dem ich nun mich neige.

Des Wissens bar,
doch des Wunsches voll:
an Liebe reich,
doch ledig der Kraft:
mögst du die Arme
nicht verachten,
die dir nur gönnen,
nicht geben mehr kann!

Mehr gabst du, Wunderfrau,
als ich zu wahren weiss.
Nicht zürne, wenn dein Lehren
mich unbelehret liess!

One lesson I know I have learnt:
that by Brünnhilde I'm loved;
one command I'll not forget:
Brünnhilde I shall remember!

Ein Wissen doch wahr ich wohl:
dass mir Brünnhilde lebt;
eine Lehre lernt' ich leicht:
Brünnhildes zu gedenken!

BRÜNNHILDE

Ah, but to prove you love me,
remember only yourself;
recall your deeds of glory;
recall that raging fire,
whose fury could not fright you,
when it blazed around my rock!

[64] Willst du mir Minne schenken,
gedenke deiner nur,
gedenke deiner Taten,
gedenk des wilden Feuers,
[4x, 45] das furchtlos du durchschrittest,
[39] da den Fels es rings umbrann.

SIEGFRIED

Brünnhilde I was winning!

[66, 64] Brünnhilde zu gewinnen!

BRÜNNHILDE

Recall how I lay on the rock,
and that long, deep sleep which bound me,
till your kiss awoke me to life.

[34] Gedenk der beschildeten Frau,
[38] die in tiefem Schlaf du fandest,
[39] der den festen Helm du erbrachst.

SIEGFRIED

Brünnhilde I awakened!

[66] Brünnhilde zu erwecken!

BRÜNNHILDE

Recall the promise
that unites us;
recall the pledges
that we plighted;
recall you love me,
and I love you:
Brünnhilde burns forever,
ever deep in your breast.

[65]   Gedenk der Eide,
die uns einen;
gedenk der Treue,
die wir tragen;
gedenk der Liebe,
der wir leben:
Brünnhilde brennt dann ewig
heilig dir in der Brust! —

She embraces Siegfried. [56]

SIEGFRIED

Love, I leave you alone,
but the flames will guard you again;
    (*He has drawn Alberich's ring from his finger and now offers it to Brünnhilde.*)
in return for all you've taught me,
let me give you this ring.
For the power of all I have done
resides within this gold.
And to gain it a dragon was killed,
who guarded the ring with his life.
Now you must guard it for me;
this ring will tell all my love!

[64] Lass ich, Liebste, dich hier
in der Lohe heiliger Hut;
ʼzum Tausche deiner Runen
[6] reich ich dir diesen Ring.
[39] Was der Taten je ich schuf,
des Tugend schliesst er ein.
[64, 21] Ich erschlug einen wilden Wurm,
der grimmig lang ihn bewacht.
Nun wahre du seine Kraft
als Weihegruss meiner Treuʼ!

BRÜNNHILDE
(*putting on the ring, in rapture*) [6, 34]

I'll guard it so long as I live!
For the ring, I give you my horse!
  Though he longs to fly
    with me through the storm clouds,
  with me
he lost his enchanted power;
  through the skies above,
  through lightning and thunder,
  no more
Grane can fly on his way;
  but wherever you lead,
  even through fire,
fearlessly Grane will bear you:
for you, my hero,

[3] Ihn geiz ich als einziges Gut!
Für den Ring nimm nun auch mein Ross!
[34]   Ging sein Lauf mit mir
einst kühn durch die Lüfte —
mit mir
verlor es die mächt'ge Art;
über Wolken hin
auf blitzenden Wettern
nicht mehr
schwingt es sich mutig des Wegs;
doch wohin du ihn führst
— sei es durchs Feuer —,
[64] grauenlos folgt dir Grane;
denn dir, o Helde,

The Prelude of (above) the Bayreuth production, 1978, with Manfred Jung as Siegfried and Gwyneth Jones as Brünnhilde (photo: Festspielleitung Bayreuth) and (below) the 1974 Kassel production with Bèla Turpinszki as Siegfried and Joy McIntyre as Brünnhilde.

you are his master.
Oh, guard him well;
he'll heed your voice:
oh, let your Grane
hear Brünnhilde's name!

soll er gehorchen!
Du hüt ihn wohl;
er hört dein Wort:
[30b] o bringe Grane
[34] oft Brünnhildes Gruss!

SIEGFRIED

So by your daring I am fired,
and all my deeds shall be your deeds!
All my battles you will choose,
all my victories you shall achieve,
when on your steed I'm mounted,
when by your shield I'm saved:
so Siegfried I am no more,
I am but Brünnhilde's arm.

[66, 34] Durch deine Tugend allein
soll so ich Taten noch wirken?
Meine Kämpfe kiesest du,
meine Siege kehren zu dir:
[64] auf deines Rosses Rücken,
in deines Schildes Schirm,
[67] nicht Siegfried acht ich mich mehr,
ich bin nur Brünnhildes Arm.

BRÜNNHILDE

I wish that Brünnhild were your soul too!   [66] O wäre Brünnhild' deine Seele!

SIEGFRIED

Her soul burns bright in my breast.   [67, 66] Durch sie entbrennt mir der Mut.

BRÜNNHILDE

Then you are Siegfried and Brünnhilde!   [66] So wärst du Siegfried und Brünnhild?

SIEGFRIED

Where I am, both are united.   [67] Wo ich bin, bergen sich beide.

BRÜNNHILDE

Then my mountain must soon be bare?   So verödet mein Felsensaal?

SIEGFRIED

Ah no, both are here in you!   [64] Vereint fasst er uns zwei!

BRÜNNHILDE
(*with great emotion*)

O heavenly rulers!
Holy immortals!
Turn your eyes
on this true, loving pair!
Apart, who can divide us?
Divided, still we are one!

[67, 65] O heilige Götter,
hehre Geschlechter!
Weidet eu'r Aug'
an dem weihvollen Paar!
Getrennt — wer will uns scheiden?
[67, 66] Geschieden — trennt es sich nie!

SIEGFRIED

Hail, O Brünnhilde,
glorious star!
Hail, love in its radiance!

[67] Heil dir, Brünnhilde,
prangender Stern!
Heil, strahlende Liebe!

BRÜNNHILDE

Hail, O Siegfried,
conquering light!
Hail, life in its radiance!

[67] Heil dir, Siegfried,
siegendes Licht!
Heil, strahlendes Leben!

BOTH

Hail! Hail! Hail! Hail!   [66, 34] Heil! Heil! Heil! Heil!

Siegfried leads the horse quickly towards the edge of the rocky slope; Brünnhilde follows him.
[64, 67, 34] Siegfried disappears with the horse down behind the rock, so that he is no longer
visible to the audience; Brünnhilde thus stands suddenly alone at the edge of the slope and
watches Siegfried as he descends. [65, 59] Siegfried's horn is heard from below. [45]
Brünnhilde listens. She steps further out on the slope, and again catches sight of Siegfried
down below; she greets him with a gesture of delight. Her joyful smiles seem to reflect the
cheerful demeanour of the departing hero. [30a, 61] The curtain falls swiftly.
[45, 13a, 61, 1c, 25, 4, 4b, 7b, 3, 6, 5]

Act One

The Hall of the Gibichungs on the Rhine. This is quite open at the back. The background itself presents an open shore as far as the river; rocky heights border the shore.

Scene One. *Gunther and Gutrune sit enthroned at one side; before them is a table with drinking vessels on it; Hagen is seated in front of the table.* [68]

GUNTHER

Now hear, Hagen;
  answer me true:
is my fame along the Rhine
worthy of Gibich's name?

Nun hör, Hagen,
  sage mir, Held:
[69] sitz ich herrlich am Rhein,
Gunther zu Gibichs Ruhm?

HAGEN

You, trueborn son,
  awaken my envy;
and she who bore us both,
fair Grimhild, taught me to honour you.

[68] Dich echt genannten
  acht ich zu neiden:
[69] die beid' uns Brüder gebar,
[6] Frau Grimhild liess mich's begreifen.

GUNTHER

Don't envy me;
  let me envy you.
I am the elder son,
yet you're the one who is wise:
half-brothers we,
  no strife between us.
And I praise you, praise your wisdom,
when I ask about my fame.

Dich neide ich:
  nicht neide mich du!
[69] Erbt' ich Erstlingsart,
[68] Weisheit ward dir allein:
  Halbbrüderzwist
  bezwang sich nie besser.
Deinem Rat nur red ich Lob,
[68] frag ich dich nach meinem Ruhm.

HAGEN

My wisdom is weak;
  your fame is not great:
I know some wondrous treasures [11a,68x]
which the Gibichungs have not yet won.

[5y] So schelt ich den Rat,
  da schlecht noch dein Ruhm:
denn hohe Güter weiss ich,
die der Gibichung noch nicht gewann.

GUNTHER

If that is so,
I blame you too.

Verschwiegst du sie,
so schelt auch ich.

HAGEN

In ripeness and strength of summer,
Gibich's children rule;
but you, Gunther, have no wife;
you, Gutrun, are unwed.

[68x]In sommerlich reifer Stärke
  seh ich Gibichs Stamm,
dich, Gunther, unbeweibt,
dich, Gutrun, ohne Mann.

Gunther and Gutrune are lost in silent thought. [68x, 11a]

GUNTHER

What woman should I wed
to make my fame more great?

Wen rätst du nun zu frein,
dass unsrem Ruhm es fromm'?

HAGEN

There's one woman,
  the noblest in the world:
a rocky crag her home;
a fire encircles the rock:
one hero will brave that fire,
then Brünnhild his bride shall be.

[34] Ein Weib weiss ich,
  das herrlichste der Welt:
[14] auf Felsen hoch ihr Sitz,
  ein Feuer umbrennt ihren Saal;
[53a]nur wer durch das Feuer bricht,
[53c]darf Brünnhildes Freier sein.

GUNTHER

Is my strength enough for the deed?

[5x, 34] Vermag das mein Mut zu bestehn?

72

Margaret Curphey as Gutrune with Aage Haugland as Hagen at ENO, 1977 (above) and (below) John Shaw as Gunther and Martti Talvela as Hagen at Covent Garden, 1970 (photos: John Garner and Reg Wilson)

HAGEN

It requires a stronger man than you.

[68x]Einem Stärkren noch ist's nur bestimmt.

GUNTHER

Who is this boldest of men?

Wer ist der streitlichste Mann?

HAGEN

Siegfried, the Wälsung son,
he is the chosen man.
The Wälsung twins
whom love united,
Siegmund and Sieglind,
created this brave noble son.
In the woods he grew to be strong;
with this man Gutrun should wed.

Siegfried, der Wälsungen Spross:
der ist der stärkste Held.
[33] Ein Zwillingspaar,
von Liebe bezwungen,
Siegmund und Sieglinde,
zeugten den echtesten Sohn.
[46] Der im Walde mächtig erwuchs,
den wünsch' ich Gutrun zum Mann.

GUTRUNE
(*beginning shyly*)

What deed did he accomplish,
to be hailed as the bravest of men?

[70] Welche Tat schuf er so tapfer,
dass als herrlichster Held er genannt?

HAGEN

At Neidhöhle
the Nibelung gold
was guarded by Fafner the giant:
Siegfried closed up
his threatening jaws,
and killed him with his conquering sword.
That great and valiant deed
has won him a hero's name.

[21] Vor Neidhöhle
den Niblungenhort
[6] bewachte ein riesiger Wurm:
[52] Siegfried schloss ihm
den freislichen Schlund,
erschlug ihm mit siegendem Schwert.
Solch ungeheurer Tat
[46] enttagte des Helden Ruhm.

GUNTHER
(*thoughtfully*)

The Nibelung hoard is famous;
I've heard men speak of the gold . . .

[6] Vom Niblungenhort vernahm ich:
er birgt den neidlichsten Schatz?

HAGEN

He who commands that gold
can bend all the world to his will.

Wer wohl ihn zu nützen wüsst',
[7b] dem neigte sich wahrlich die Welt.

GUNTHER

And Siegfried won it himself?

[3] Und Siegfried hat ihn erkämpft?

HAGEN

Slaves are the Niblungs to him.

[5] Knecht sind die Niblungen ihm.

GUNTHER

And Brünnhild must fall to his might?

[27] Und Brünnhild gewänne nur er?

HAGEN

He alone can pass through the flame.

[34] Keinem andren wiche die Brunst.

GUNTHER
(*rises impatiently from his seat.*)

Then why do you mention this bride?
And why arouse my hopes
with dreams of a treasure
that cannot be mine?

Wie weckst du Zweifel und Zwist!
Was ich nicht zwingen soll,
darnach zu verlangen
machst du mir Lust?

He paces the hall in agitation. [69] *Hagen, without leaving his seat, stops Gunther with a mysterious gesture as he approaches him.* [18, 71]

HAGEN

What if Siegfried

Brächte Siegfried

should win the bride —
might he not give her to you?

die Braut dir heim,
wär' dann nicht Brünnhilde dein?

GUNTHER
(*turns away again in doubt and discontent.*)

But how could I urge this man
to win the bride for me?

Was zwänge den frohen Mann,
für mich die Braut zu frein?

HAGEN
(*as before*)

Your word would easily urge him,
were but Gutrun his wife.

Ihn zwänge bald deine Bitte,
bänd' ihn Gutrun zuvor.

GUTRUNE

You mock me, cruel Hagen,
for how could Siegfried love me?
  If he is the bravest
  of men in the world,
then earth's most lovely women
long since have known his love.

[72] Du Spötter, böser Hagen,
wie sollt' ich Siegfried binden?
  Ist er der herrlichste
  Held der Welt,
[70] der Erde holdeste Frauen
friedeten längst ihn schon.

HAGEN
(*leaning over confidentially to Gutrune*)

Remember that drink in the chest;

[72] Gedenk des Trankes im Schrein;
(*more secretly*)

and trust in me; I know its power.
That hero for whom you long,
he can be conquered by you.

vertraue mir, der ihn gewann;
den Helden, des du verlangst,
[7b,11a] bindet er liebend an dich.

(*Gunther has again come to the table and, leaning on it, listens attentively.*)

Now let our Siegfried come:
we'll give him the magical drink;
he'll forget all women but you;
the past will fade from his mind;
all memory he will have lost.
  Now tell me,
how like you Hagen's plan?

[27] Träte nun Siegfried ein,
[72] genöss' er des würzigen Tranks,
[18,11a] dass vor dir ein Weib er ersah,
dass je ein Weib ihm genaht,
[71] vergessen müsst' er des ganz.
  Nun redet,
[5y] wie dünkt euch Hagens Rat?

GUNTHER
(*starting up with animation*) [68]

I praise our mother Grimhild,
who bore a son so wise!

Gepriesen sei Grimhild,
[69] die uns den Bruder gab!

GUTRUNE

And will Siegfried pass this way?

[72] Möcht' ich Siegfried je ersehn!

GUNTHER

How can we draw him here?

[23] Wie fänden wir ihn auf?

A horn sounds from the background on the left. Hagen listens. [45, 73x]

HAGEN

Merrily seeking
adventures and fame,
he sails the Rhine,
he roams the world:
his journey will bring him this way,
to the Gibich's home on the Rhine.

Jagt er auf Taten
wonnig umher,
zum engen Tann
wird ihm die Welt:
wohl stürmt er in rastloser Jagd
auch zu Gibichs Strand an den Rhein.

GUNTHER

Gladly I'd welcome him here.

Willkommen hiess' ich ihn gern.

(*The horn sounds closer, though still distant.* [45] *Both listen.*)

On the Rhine I can hear a horn.

[68x, 69] Von Rhein her tönt das Horn.

75

(has gone to the shore; he looks downstream, and calls back:) [5x]

I see a vessel — man and horse!	[72] In einem Nachen Held und Ross!
Ha! Hear him blowing his horn!	[45, 4] Der bläst so munter das Horn!
With a powerful stroke,	Ein gemächlicher Schlag,
yet with leisurely ease,	wie von müssiger Hand,
he drives the boat,	treibt jach den Kahn
braving the stream:	wider den Strom;
such strength in his arms	so rüstiger Kraft
as he plies the oars!	in des Ruders Schwung
Yes, it is he	[27] rühmt sich nur der,
who destroyed the giant.	der den Wurm erschlug.
Siegfried's coming, he and no other!	Siegfried ist es, sicher kein andrer!

[6]

GUNTHER

Will he go by?	Jagt er vorbei?

HAGEN

(calling towards the river through his cupped hands)

Hoiho! You boatman,	Hoiho! Wohin,
where are you bound?	du heitrer Held?

SIEGFRIED'S VOICE

(in the distance, from the river)

To Gunther, son of Gibich.	Zu Gibichs starkem Sohne.

HAGEN

His hall awaits you; be welcome here.	[69, 72] Zu seiner Halle entbiet ich dich.

(Siegfried appears at the shore in a boat.)

This way! Here tie the boat!	Hieher! Hier lege an!

Scene Two. *Siegfried brings his boat alongside and, after Hagen has made it fast with a cable, leaps on shore, with his horse.*

HAGEN

Hail! Siegfried, welcome here!	[23] Heil! Siegfried, teurer Held!

Gunther has joined Hagen on the shore. From the throne, Gutrune looks at Siegfried in astonishment. [72] Gunther prepares to offer friendly greetings. All are fixed in silent mutual contemplation.

SIEGFRIED

(leaning on his horse, remains quietly standing by the boat.)

Which is Gibich's son?	[39] Wer ist Gibichs Sohn?

GUNTHER

Gunther, I whom you seek.	[69] Gunther, ich, den du suchst.

SIEGFRIED

Gunther is praised	[39] Dich hört' ich rühmen
along the Rhine:	weit am Rhein:
now fight with me,	nun ficht mit mir
or be my friend!	oder sei mein Freund!

GUNTHER

Come in peace!	Lass den Kampf!
And be welcome!	Sei wilkommen!

SIEGFRIED

(looking around calmly)

Who'll care for my horse?	[34] Wo berg ich mein Ross?

I'll give him rest.   Ich biet ihm Rast.

SIEGRIED
(turning to Hagen)

You called me Siegfried: [23] Du riefst mich Siegfried:
how did you know?   sahst du mich schon?

HAGEN

I knew when I saw   [39] Ich kannte dich nur
your mighty strength.   an deiner Kraft.

SIEGFRIED
(as he gives the horse to Hagen)

Take care of my Grane: [34, 65] Wohl hüte mir Grane!
in all the world   Du hieltest nie
you'll never find   [66] von edlerer Zucht
a horse more noble than he.   am Zaume ein Ross.

*Hagen leads the horse away to the right, behind the hall. While Siegfried looks thoughtfully
after him, Gutrune, at a gesture of Hagen's unnoticed by Siegfried, goes out through a door on
the left leading to her room. Gunther advances into the hall with Siegfried, inviting him to
accompany him. [74]*

GUNTHER

I welcome you, my friend,   Begrüsse froh, oh Held,
within the home of my fathers;   die Halle meines Vaters;
the hall you stand in,   wohin du schreitest,
and all you see,   was du ersiehst,
freely you may command them;   das achte nun dein eigen:
share in my birthright,   dein ist mein Erbe,
land and men: Land und Leut' —
by my life let me swear it!   hilf, mein Leib, meinem Eide!
Me, too, you may command!   [74] Mich selbst geb ich zum Mann.

SIEGFRIED

No land nor men have I to give, [69] Nicht Land noch Leute biete ich,
no father's house or hall: [33] noch Vaters Haus und Hof:
all my birthright   einzig erbt' ich
my sturdy limbs,   den eignen Leib:
useless things when I'm dead.   [58] lebend zehr ich den auf.
Yet a sword have I;   [51] Nur ein Schwert hab ich,
I forged it myself: [27, 17] selbst geschmiedet:
by my sword let me swear then!   [74] hilf, mein Schwert, meinem Eide!
Body and sword shall be yours.   Das biet ich mit mir zum Bund.

HAGEN
(has returned, and now stands behind Siegfried.)

But the Niblung gold, they say, [20, 17] Doch des Nibelungenhortes
belongs now to you.   nennt die Märe dich Herrn?

SIEGFRIED
(turning round to Hagen)

That treasure I quite forgot; [4, 17] Des Schatzes vergass ich fast:
I hold it of little worth!   so schätz ich sein müss'ges Gut!
I left it lying in a cavern,   [21] In einer Höhle liess ich's liegen,
where a dragon once did dwell.   wo ein Wurm es einst bewacht'.

HAGEN

And took no gold away?   [4, 17] Und nichts entnahmst du ihm?

SIEGFRIED
(indicating the steel chainmail hanging from his belt)

Only this: I know not its use!   Dies Gewirk, unkund seiner Kraft.

The Tarnhelm truly,	Den Tarnhelm kenn ich,
the Niblung's most wonderful work:	der Niblungen künstliches Werk:
for this, when placed on your head,	[18] er taugt, bedeckt er dein Haupt,
can transform you to any shape;	dir zu tauschen jede Gestalt;
and take you to any place:	verlangt dich's an fernsten Ort,
you just wish, and you are there!	er entführt flugs dich dahin.
What else did you take from the cave?	Sonst nichts entnahmst du dem Hort?

SIEGFRIED

Just a ring.	[6] Einen Ring.

HAGEN

And where is it now?	Den hütest du wohl?

SIEGFRIED

Kept safe on a fair woman's hand.	[66] Den hütet ein hehres Weib.

HAGEN
(aside)

Brünnhild's! [68]	Brünnhild! . . .

GUNTHER

Siegfried, there is naught you need give me.	[74] Nicht, Siegfried, sollst du mir tauschen:
I could make no fit return	Tand gäb' ich für dein Geschmeid',
even if you took all I have;	nähmst all mein Gut du dafür.
out of friendship, you I shall serve.	Ohn' Entgelt dien ich dir gern.

Hagen has gone to Gutrune's door and now opens it. Gutrune comes out and approaches Siegfried, carrying a filled drinking-horn. [75]

GUTRUNE

Welcome, O guest,	Willkommen, Gast,
to Gibich's house!	in Gibichs Haus!
Let his daughter give you this drink.	Seine Tochter reicht dir den Trank.

SIEGFRIED
(bows to her politely and takes the horn. Holding it up thoughtfully, he says softly:)

Though I forget	[59] Vergäss' ich alles,
all else that you gave,	was du mir gabst,
one holy lesson	von einer Lehre
I shall recall:	lass ich doch nie!
this drink, the first	[56] Den ersten Trunk
I taste as lover,	zu treuer Minne,
Brünnhild, I drink to you!	Brünnhilde, bring ich dir!

(He raises the horn and takes a long draught. [71] He returns the horn to Gutrune, who casts down her eyes before him in shame and confusion. [75] Siegfried fixes his gaze on her with suddenly inflamed passion.)

Those eyes with a flash	Die so mit dem Blitz
set fire to my heart;	den Blick du mir sengst,
why lower your glorious gaze?	was senkst du dein Auge vor mir?

(Gutrune, blushing, raises her eyes to his face.)

Ah, fairest maid!	Ha, schönstes Weib!
Close them again;	Schliesse den Blick;
the heart in my breast	das Herz in der Brust
burns in their beams;	brennt mir sein Strahl:
the blood in my veins is kindled	zu feurigen Strömen fühl ich
to scorching fiery streams!	[5b] ihn zehrend zünden mein Blut!

(with trembling voice)

Gunther, what is the name of your sister?	[72] Gunther, wie heisst deine Schwester?

GUNTHER

Gutrune.	[75] Gutrune.

SIEGFRIED
(softly)

Do I read a welcome	Sind's gute Runen,
there in the shining eyes of Gutrun?	die ihrem Aug' ich entrate?

(Ardently and impetuously he seizes Gutrune's hand.)

With your brother I offered to serve;	Deinem Bruder bot ich mich zum Mann:
his pride refused my aid.	[74] der Stolze schlug mich aus;
Will you, like him, reject my plea?	trügst du, wie er, mir Übermut,
Or may I serve with you?	böt' ich mich dir zum Bund?

Gutrune involuntarily catches Hagen's eye. [68x] *She bows her head and, with a gesture as if she felt herself unworthy, she leaves the hall with faltering steps.* [75]

SIEGFRIED
(watched closely by Hagen and Gunther, gazes after Gutrune as if bewitched [23]; then, without turning round, he asks:)

Gunther, have you a wife?	Hast du, Gunther, ein Weib?

GUNTHER

No wife have I yet;	[74] Nicht freit' ich noch,
the wife I long for	und einer Frau
will be hard to find,	[34] soll ich mich schwerlich freun!
for I have set my desire	[5b] Auf eine setzt' ich den Sinn,
on a maid whom I cannot win!	[68] die kein Rat mir je gewinnt.

SIEGFRIED
(turns with animation to Gunther.) [69]

Whom can you not win,	Was wär' dir versagt,
with me to help?	[58] steh ich zu dir?

GUNTHER

A rocky crag her home;	[14] Auf Felsen hoch ihr Sitz;
a fire surrounds the rock —	ein Feuer umbrennt den Saal —

SIEGFRIED
(breaking in hastily in astonishment)

'A rocky crag her home;	'Auf Felsen hoch ihr Sitz;
a fire surrounds the rock' . . .?	ein Feuer umbrennt den Saal' . . .?

GUNTHER

One hero will brave the fire —	[53a]Nur wer durch das Feuer bricht —

SIEGFRIED
(striving with intense effort to remember something)

'One hero will brave the fire' . . .?	'Nur wer durch das Feuer bricht' . . .?

GUNTHER

Then Brünnhild his bride shall be.	[53d] — darf Brünnhildes Freier sein.

(Siegfried shows by a gesture that at the mention of Brünnhilde's name his memory has quite faded.)

I dare not set foot on that mountain;	[71] Nun darf ich den Fels nicht erklimm'en;
those flames would make me fear!	das Feuer verglimmt mir nie!

SIEGFRIED
(comes to himself from his dreamy state and turns to Gunther with cheerful self-confidence.)
[13a, 72]

I fear not the flames,	Ich — fürchte kein Feuer,
and for you I shall win the bride;	für dich frei ich die Frau,
for your friend am I,	[18] denn dein Mann bin ich,
and my strength is yours,	und mein Mut ist dein,
if I can have Gutrun as wife.	[75] gewinn ich mir Gutrun zum Weib.

GUNTHER

Gutrun I'll give to you gladly.	Gutrune gönn ich dir gerne.

Siegfried and Gunther pledge their loyalty to each other: (above) Thomas Stewart as Gunther, Gottlob Frick as Hagen and Wolfgang Windgassen as Siegfried at Covent Garden in 1964 and (below) Alberto Remedios as Siegfried, Aage Haugland as Hagen and Norman Welsby as Gunther at ENO in 1976 (photos: Donald Southern, Reg Wilson)

	SIEGFRIED
Brünnhilde then is yours.	[34] Brünnhilde bring ich dir.

SIEGFRIED

Brünnhilde then is yours.　　　　　　　　[34] Brünnhilde bring ich dir.

GUNTHER

But how will you deceive her?　　　　　Wie willst du sie täuschen?

SIEGFRIED

By the Tarnhelm's art　　　　　　　　[18]　Durch des Tarnhelms Trug
I can be changed into you.　　　　　　　tausch ich mir deine Gestalt.

GUNTHER

Then let us swear by a vow!　　　　　So stelle Eide zum Schwur!

SIEGFRIED

Blood brotherhood　　　　　　　　　[76a]　Blut-Brüderschaft
joins us as one!　　　　　　　　　　　schwöre ein Eid!

Hagen fills a drinking-horn with fresh wine, [23, 9a] and holds it out to Siegfried and Gunther, who cut their arms with their swords and hold them for a moment over the top of the horn. [13a, 27, 69] Both lay two fingers on the horn, which Hagen continues to hold between them.

[68x, 9a]

SIEGFRIED

Flourishing life's　　　　　　　　　[76b]　Blühenden Lebens
refreshing blood　　　　　　　　　　　labendes Blut
we have shed in this horn.　　　　　　träufelt' ich in den Trank.

GUNTHER

Bravely blended　　　　　　　　　　[76b]　Bruder-brünstig
brotherly love,　　　　　　　　　　　mutig gemischt
born in the drink from our blood!　　blüh im Trank unser Blut.

BOTH

Truth I swear to my friend!　　　　　[76c]Treue trink ich dem Freund.
Fair and free,　　　　　　　　　　　[76d]　Froh und frei
the blood is our bond;　　　　　　　　entblühe dem Bund
blood-brotherhood here!　　　　　　　[76a]Blut-Brüderschaft heut!

[68x, 9a]

GUNTHER

If one friend should be false —　　　[76e]Bricht ein Bruder den Bund —

SIEGFRIED

If one friend should betray —　　　　Trügt den Treuen der Freund —

BOTH

then not drops of blood —　　　　　Was in Tropfen heut
all his life blood　　　　　　　　　　hold wir tranken,
shall flow in streams from his veins;　in Strahlen ström' es dahin,
traitors so must atone!　　　　　　　[76f] fromme Sühne dem Freund!

GUNTHER
(drinks and hands the horn to Siegfried.) [23, 9a]

I swear to be true!　　　　　　　　So — biet ich den Bund.

SIEGFRIED

I swear to be true!　　　　　　　　[76a, 79] So — trink ich dir Treu'!

He drinks and holds out the empty drinking-horn to Hagen. Hagen strikes the horn into two with his sword [68x, 9a]. Gunther and Siegfried join hands. [76a, 74]

SIEGFRIED
(observes Hagen, who has stood behind him during the oath.) [72]

But you did not join us in our oath!　[75] Was nahmst du am Eide nicht teil?

81

My blood would spoil all your drink;   [76e]Mein Blut verdürb' euch den Trank;
my blood's not pure   [76a, 17, 73]   nicht fliesst mir's echt
and noble like yours;   [6]   und edel wie euch;
stubborn and cold,   störrisch und kalt
slow to stir,   stockt's in mir;
my blood flows slowly and strangely: [7b] nicht will's die Wange mir röten.
I take no part   Drum bleib ich fern
in fiery vows.   vom feurigen Bund.

GUNTHER
(*to Siegfried*)

Leave this unhappy man!   [68] Lass den unfrohen Mann!

SIEGFRIED
(*takes up his shield again.*) [34]

Now on our way!   [72]   Frisch auf die Fahrt!
There lies my boat: [68]   Dort liegt mein Schiff;
swiftly sail to the mountain!   [13a]schnell führt es zum Felsen.
For a night I'll leave you;   [18]   Eine Nacht am Ufer
then, when I've won her,   harrst du im Nachen;
your bride you shall bring home!   die Frau fährst du dann heim.

He turns to leave, and beckons to Gunther to follow him.

GUNTHER

Will you not rest awhile?   Rastest du nicht zuvor?

SIEGFRIED

When you've gained her, then I'll rest.   Um die Rückkehr ist mir's jach!

He goes to the shore to cast off the boat.

GUNTHER

You, Hagen, keep watch over the palace!   Du, Hagen, bewache die Halle!

He follows Siegfried to the shore. Siegfried and Gunther, after they have laid their weapons in the boat, put up the sail and make all ready for departure; Hagen takes up his spear and shield. Gutrune appears at the door of her room just as Siegfried pushes off the boat, which floats at once into midstream. [72, 68, 34, 13a]

GUTRUNE

So fast! Where have they gone to?   Wohin eilen die Schnellen?

HAGEN
(*while he slowly seats himself in front of the hall with shield and spear*)

They've sailed — Brünnhild they'll find. [34, 76e] Zu Schiff — Brünnhild zu frein.

GUTRUNE

Siegfried?   Siegfried?

HAGEN

See, see his haste!   Sieh, wie's ihn treibt,
He's eager to win you!   [75] zum Weib dich zu gewinnen!

GUTRUNE

Siegfried — mine!   Siegfried — mein!
She returns to her room in excitement. Siegfried has seized an oar and with its strokes he drives the boat down the stream so that it is quickly lost to view. [4, 45, 75]

HAGEN
(*sits motionless, leaning his back against the doorpost of the hall.*)
[22, 68x, 45]

I sit here and wait,   Hier sitz ich zur Wacht,
watching the house,   wahre den Hof,
guarding the hall from the foe.   [5, 5b] wehre die Halle dem Feind.

Gibich's son		Gibichs Sohne
is borne by the wind,		wehet der Wind,
away to his wooing he's gone.		auf Werben fährt er dahin.
His ship is steered		Ihm führt das Steuer
by his fearless friend,	[39]	ein starker Held,
who'll brave the fire in his stead;	[5, 5b]	Gefahr ihm will er bestehn.
and he will bring	[71, 34]	Die eigne Braut
his bride to the Rhine;		ihm bringt er zum Rhein;
with her, he brings me the ring!	[68x, 7b]	mir aber bringt er — den Ring!
You sons of freedom,	[3]	Ihr freien Söhne,
joyful companions,		frohe Gesellen,
merrily sail on your way!		segelt nur lustig dahin!
Though you despise me,		Dünkt er euch niedrig,
you'll serve me soon,	[8, 3]	ihr dient ihm doch,
the Niblung's son.		des Niblungen Sohn.

A curtain, attached to the front of the hall, closes, and cuts off the stage from the audience.
[5, 68x, 6, 45, 39, 9a, 81, 73, 65, 59, 23]

Scene Three. *The Rocky Height, as in the Prelude. Brünnhilde is sitting at the entrance to the cave, in silent contemplation of Siegfried's ring.* [71] *Overcome by joyful memories, she covers it with kisses. Distant thunder is heard; she looks up and listens.* [34] *Then she turns again to the ring. A flash of lightning. Brünnhilde listens again and looks into the distance, where a dark thundercloud is seen approaching the rocky height.*

BRÜNNHILDE

Sounds I once knew so well		Altgewohntes Geräusch
steal on my ears from the distance.		raunt meinem Ohr die Ferne.
I see it —		Ein Lutross jagt
there's a Valkyrie horse:		im Laufe daher;
through the clouds it is speeding		auf der Wolke fährt es
here to my rock.		wetternd zum Fels.
Who dares to seek me again?		Wer fand mich Einsame auf?

WALTRAUTE'S VOICE
(from the distance)

Brünnhilde! Sister!	[35]	Brünnhilde! Schwester!
Wake from your slumber!		Schläfst oder wachst du?

BRÜNNHILDE
(leaping up)

Waltraute's call,	Waltrautes Ruf,
so joyful the sound!	so wonnig mir kund!

(calling off stage)

Welcome sister!	Kommst du, Schwester?
Boldly flying to my rock!	Schwingst dich kühn zu mir her?

(She hastens to the edge of the rocks.)

There in the wood —	Dort im Tann
you know the place —	— dir noch vertraut —
leap from your horse,	steige vom Ross
and leave him safely to rest.	und stell den Renner zur Rast!

(She runs into the wood, from which a loud sound like a thunderclap is heard. Brünnhilde comes back, very excited, with Waltraute; she remains in joyful excitement, without observing Waltraute's anxious fear.)

You've come to me?	Kommst du zu mir?
Are you so bold,	Bist du so kühn,
daring to seek me,	magst ohne Grauen
Brünnhild, here on her rock?	Brünnhild bieten den Gruss?

WALTRAUTE

You alone	Einzig dir nur
are the cause of my haste!	galt meine Eil'!

For love of me, for Brünnhilde's sake,   So wagtest du, Brünnhild zulieb,
Wotan's command, you've broken?   Walvaters Bann zu brechen?
Or perhaps — oh say —   Oder wie — o sag —
can it be true? —   wär' wider mich
Wotan's mind is changed?   Wotans Sinn erweicht?
  When against his anger   [77] Als dem Gott entgegen
  Siegmund I guarded,   Siegmund ich schützte,
  my deed — I know it —   fehlend — ich weiss es —
my deed fulfilled his desire.   erfüllt' ich doch seinen Wunsch.
  And I know that his anger   Dass sein Zorn sich verzogen,
  is no more.   weiss ich auch;
For although I was bound in sleep,   denn verschloss er mich gleich in Schlaf,
left all alone on the rock,   fesselt' er mich auf den Fels,
meant as a prize for the man   wies er dem Mann mich zur Magd,
who might pass and wake me to life,   der am Weg mich fänd' und erweckt' —
  to my sad entreaty   [41] meiner bangen Bitte
  he granted grace: doch gab er Gunst:
  with ravening fire   [34,13a] mit zehrendem Feuer
  he surrounded the rock,   umgab er den Fels,
so that none but a hero could pass.   [41] dem Zagen zu wehren den Weg.
  So my blessing   So zur Seligsten
  I gained by my sentence: schuf mich die Strafe:
  the noblest of men   [59, 39] der herrlichste Held
  has won me as wife!   gewann mich zum Weib!
  Blessed by his love,   In seiner Liebe
in light and laughter I live.   leucht und lach ich heut auf.
(She embraces Waltraute, who attempts with anxious impatience to restrain her.) [59, 35, 34]
Ah, were you drawn here by my love?   [77] Lockte dich, Schwester, mein Los?
  You've come to join me,   An meiner Wonne
  gaze on my rapture,   willst du dich weiden,
share all that I have won?   teilen, was mich betraf?

WALTRAUTE
(vehemently)

  Share all the frenzy   Teilen den Taumel,
that has maddened your brain?   der dich Törin erfasst?
In anguish and dread I have come,   Ein andres bewog mich in Angst,
defying Wotan's command.   zu brechen Wotans Gebot.

Brünnhilde here first observes with surprise Waltraute's extreme agitation.

BRÜNNHILDE

  Anguish and fear   [77] Angst und Furcht
  I read in your features!   fesseln dich Arme?
So the god has pardoned me not?   So verzieh der Strenge noch nicht?
You still are afraid of his wrath?   Du zagst vor des Strafenden Zorn?

WALTRAUTE
(gloomily)

  If still I feared him,   [36a] Dürft' ich ihn fürchten,
I should have nothing else to fear!   meiner Angst fänd' ich ein End'!

BRÜNNHILDE

Sister, I do not understand!   Staunend versteh ich dich nicht!

WALTRAUTE

  Calm your frenzy,   Wehre der Wallung,
pay good heed to my words!   achtsam höre mich an!
  To Walhall that dread   Nach Walhall wieder
  must make me return,   treibt mich die Angst
which from Walhall drove me away.   die von Walhall hieher mich trieb.

What harm can assail the immortals?		Was ist's mit den ewigen Göttern?

WALTRAUTE

Hear me in calm, and I will tell you!		Höre mit Sinn, was ich dir sage!
Since you and he were parted,		Seit er von dir geschieden,
we've fought no more battles		zur Schlacht nicht mehr
for Wotan.		schickte uns Wotan;
Dazed and doubting,		irr und ratlos
we Valkyries rode to the field —		ritten wir ängstlich zu Heer;
Walhall's valiant heroes		Walhalls mutige Helden
all left leaderless!		mied Walvater.
Alone on his horse,	[25]	Einsam zu Ross,
without peace or rest,	[36b]	ohne Ruh noch Rast,
through the world as a wanderer he rode.		durchschweift' er als Wandrer die Welt.
But then he came home;	[8]	Jüngst kehrte er heim;
in his hand	[9a]	in der Hand hielt er
his sacred spear was splintered,	[8]	seines Speeres Splitter:
that spear which a hero had shattered.		die hatte ein Held ihm geschlagen.
He gave a sign:		Mit stummem Wink
Walhall's heroes		Walhalls Edle
went on their way —		wies er zum Forst,
the World Ash-tree was fated.	[63, 8]	die Weltesche zu fällen.
The sacred branches		Des Stammes Scheite
he bade them break,		hiess er sie schichten
then pile in a heap		zu ragendem Hauf
all round the glorious hall.		rings um der Seligen Saal.
The holy clan	[8, 60]	Der Götter Rat
came as he called them;		liess er berufen;
and Wotan, on high,		den Hochsitz nahm
took his place.		heilig er ein:
By his side		ihm zu Seiten
in fear and dismay they assembled;		hiess er die Bangen sich setzen,
in ranks around the hall		in Ring und Reih'
he stationed his heroes.		die Hall' erfüllen die Helden.
He sits there,		So sitzt er,
speaks no word,	[38]	sagt kein Wort,
enthroned in silence,		auf hehrem Sitze
stern and sad;		stumm und ernst,
the spear in splinters		des Speeres Splitter
grasped in his hand.		fest in der Faust;
Holda's apples	[16]	Holdas Äpfel
tastes he no more.		rührt er nicht an.
Fearful and trembling,	[8]	Staunen und Bangen
the gods look on in silence.		binden starr die Götter.
He has sent his ravens	[5x]	Seine Raben beide
forth on their journeys;		sandt' er auf Reise:
when they return		kehrten die einst
and bring the news he awaits,		mit guter Kunde zurück,
then for the last time	[4]	dann noch einmal,
a smile of joy		zum letztenmal,
will shine on the face of the god.		lächelte ewig der Gott.
Round his knees are gathered,	[9a]	Seine Knie umwindend,
in anguish, we Valkyries;		liegen wir Walküren;
blind, he will not heed		blind bleibt er
our entreaties;		den flehenden Blicken;
and all are afraid,		uns alle verzehrt
filled with an endless dismay.		Zagen und endlose Angst.
Then on his breast		An seine Brust
I wept in my sorrow;		presst' ich mich weinend:
his glance grew more mild;		da brach sich sein Blick —
he remembered, Brünnhilde, you!	[44]	er gedachte, Brünnhilde, dein!
He sighed in grief,		Tief seufzt' er auf,

closed his eye,	schloss das Auge,
and deep in dreaming, [4x]	und wie im Traume
whispered these words:	raunt' er das Wort:
'If once the Rhine's fair daughters [6]	'Des tiefen Rheines Töchtern
win back their ring from Brünnhild again, [7b]	gäbe den Ring sie wieder zurück,
then the curse will pass; [23]	von des Fluches Last
she will save both god and the world!' [4x, 8d]	erlöst wär' Gott und Welt!'
So I took thought; [9a]	Da sann ich nach:
I left our father,	von seiner Seite
and through the silence	durch stumme Reihen
stole from the hall;	stahl ich mich fort;
in secret haste	in heimlicher Hast
I mounted my horse,	bestieg ich mein Ross
and rode the storm to your rock.	und ritt im Sturme zu dir.
Hear, O sister,	Dich, o Schwester,
and grant my prayer:	bechwör ich nun:
you, you alone	was du vermagst,
can help in our need!	vollend' es dein Mut!
End our remorse and our grief!	Ende der Ewigen Qual!

She has thrown herself at Brünnhilde's feet. [9a]

BRÜNNHILDE
(*quietly*)

These tales of evil fancies	Welch banger Träume Mären
hold no meaning for me!	meldest du Traurige mir!
The gods and Walhall's [8a]	Der Götter heiligem
cloudy splendours,	Himmelsnebel
I, poor fool, have escaped;	bin ich Törin enttaucht:
so how can Walhall concern me?	nicht fass ich, was ich erfahre.
Strange and wild, [78]	Wirr und wüst
all that you say:	scheint mir dein Sinn;
and in your eyes,	in deinem Aug',
so wild and weary,	so übermüde,
gleam flames of desire.	glänzt flackernde Glut.
With pallid features,	Mit blasser Wange,
unhappy sister,	du bleiche Schwester,
oh tell me, what would you ask?	was willst du Wilde von mir?

WALTRAUTE
(*vehemently*) [6]

Upon your hand, the ring,	An deiner Hand, der Ring,
that ring! Hear my advice:	er ist's; hör meinen Rat:
for Wotan, cast it away!	für Wotan wirf ihn von dir!

BRÜNNHILDE

The ring? My ring?	Den Ring? Von mir?

WALTRAUTE

Let the Rhinemaidens have it again! [5x]	Den Rheintöchtern gib ihn zurück!

BRÜNNHILDE

The Rhinemaidens? — I? — the ring?	Den Rheintöchtern, ich, den Ring?
Siegfried's pledge to me?	Siegfrieds Liebespfand?
Your words are madness!	Bist du von Sinnen?

WALTRAUTE

Hear me, hear my despair! [5b, 6]	Hör mich, hör meine Angst!
The world's future	Der Welt Unheil
all depends on the ring.	haftet sicher an ihm.
Cast it from you,	Wirf ihn von dir,
down in the waters;	fort in die Welle!
Walhall's grief shall be ended,	Walhalls Elend zu enden,
when you cast it back in the Rhine.	den verfluchten wirf in die Flut!

86

Ha! Learn then what it means to me!
  How can you grasp it,
  unfeeling maid!
More than Walhall's pleasures,
more than the fame of the gods,
  more is this ring.
One glance at its shining gold,
one flash of its holy fire
  I hold dearer
  than all the gods'
eternal, loveless delights.
  The shine of this gold
tells me that Siegfried loves me!
Siegfried loves me!
O joy that transfigures my being!
Love lives in the ring.

  Go home to the sacred
  clan of the gods!
And of my ring
you may give them this reply:
My love shall last while I live,
my ring in life shall not leave me!
  Fall first in ruins
Walhall's glorious pride!

Ha, weisst du, was er mir ist?
  Wie kannst du's fassen,
  fühllose Maid!
[6] Mehr als Walhalls Wonne,
mehr als der Ewigen Ruhm
  ist mir der Ring:
ein Blick auf sein helles Gold,
ein Blitz aus dem hehren Glanz
  gilt mir werter
  als aller Götter
ewig währendes Glück!
[56] Denn selig aus ihm
leuchtet mir Siegfrieds Liebe,
  Siegfrieds Liebe!
[66] O liess' sich die Wonne dir sagen!
[59] Sie — wahrt mir der Reif.

[78] Geh hin zu der Götter
  heiligem Rat!
Von meinem Ringe
  raune ihnen zu:
[7] Die Liebe liesse ich nie,
mir nähmen nie sie die Liebe,
[8a] stürzt' auch in Trümmern
Walhalls strahlende Pracht!

This is your loyalty?
  And to sorrow,
you cruelly abandon your sister?

[9b] Dies deine Treue?
[23] So in Trauer
entlässest du lieblos die Schwester?

Back to your horse!
Fly on your way!
The ring remains on my hand!

[9b] Schwinge dich fort!
[23] Fliege zu Ross!
Den Reif entführst du mir nicht!

Sorrow! Sorrow!
Woe my sister!
Woe to Walhall, woe!

[5x] Wehe! Wehe!
Weh dir, Schwester!
Walhalls Göttern weh!

She rushes away. A stormy thundercloud soon rises from the wood. [34, 35]

(*as she watches the thundercloud disappear in the distance with flashes of brilliant lightning*)

Borne by the wind,
through flashing stormclouds,
fly on your way:
to me you need not return!

Blitzend Gewölk,
vom Wind getragen,
stürme dahin:
zu mir nie steure mehr her!

(*Evening has fallen. From below, the light of the fire gradually grows brighter. Brünnhilde looks quietly out on the landscape.*) [14]

Dark shades of evening
veil the heavens;
  brightly blazes
the guardian fire of the rock.

Abendlich Dämmern
deckt den Himmel;
  heller leuchtet
die hütende Lohe herauf.

(*The fire-light approaches from below. Tongues of flame, growing continually brighter, dart up over the rocky edge.*) [13b]

  The flames leap wildly,
and why do they flare up on high?
  The mountain peak
is walled by a rampart of flame.

Was leckt so wütend
[13a]die lodernde Welle zum Wall?
  Zur Felsenspitze
wälzt sich der feurige Schwall.

(*Siegfried's horn-call sounds from below.* [39] *Brünnhilde listens, and starts up in delight.*)

Siegfried!
Siegfried returns,
and his call rings in my ears!

Siegfried!
[45] Siegfried zurück!
Seinen Ruf sendet er her!

87

| Ah! Ah, I must meet him! | Auf! — Auf, ihm entgegen! |
| I greet my god once more! | [39] In meines Gottes Arm! |

She hastens to the rocky parapet in the utmost joy. [45] Flames shoot up from below; Siegfried leaps forward onto a high rock: the flames immediately draw back and once again only flicker on the lower slopes. On his head he wears the Tarnhelm, which covers the upper half of his face except for his eyes; he appears in Gunther's form.

BRÜNNHILDE
(shrinking in terror)

| Betrayed! Who dares come here? | [18] Verrat! — Wer drang zu mir? |

She rushes to the foreground, and gazes at Siegfried in speechless astonishment.

SIEGFRIED
(remaining on the rock at the back, leans on his shield, motionless, observing her for a while. [71, 69] Then, in a feigned — and deeper — voice, he addresses her.)

Brünnhild! Your husband comes;	[18] Brünnhild! Ein Freier kam,
I have sought you through the flames.	den dein Feuer nicht geschreckt.
I claim you as my wife:	[71] Dich werb ich nun zum Weib:
now you belong to me!	[69] du folge willig mir!

BRÜNNHILDE
(trembling violently)

Who is the man	Wer ist der Mann,
who dares to come here	der das vermochte,
where the bravest alone may climb?	[18] was dem Stärksten nur bestimmt?

SIEGFRIED
(as before)

| A hero who will tame you, | [71] Ein Helde, der dich zähmt, |
| if you resist my might. | [69] bezwingt Gewalt dich nur. |

BRÜNNHILDE
(seized with fear)

A demon	Ein Unhold schwang sich
come to usurp the rock!	auf jenen Stein!
An eagle has flown here	[5x] Ein Aar kam geflogen,
to tear me to pieces!	mich zu zerfleischen!
Who are you, dreadful one?	Wer bist du, Schrecklicher?
Are you a mortal?	[18] Stammst du von Menschen?
Are you a demon	Kommst du von Hellas
sent from hell?	nächtlichem Heer?

SIEGFRIED
(as before, beginning with a slightly trembling voice, but continuing more confidently)

A Gibichung am I,	[71, 68] Ein Gibichung bin ich,
and Gunther is my name;	[69] und Gunther heisst der Held,
now, maid, you follow me.	dem, Frau, du folgen sollst.

BRÜNNHILDE
(breaking out in despair)

Wotan! You cruel,	Wotan! Ergrimmter,
merciless god!	grausamer Gott!
Ah! Now my sentence	[78] Weh! Nun erseh ich
I understand!	der Strafe Sinn;
To shame and sorrow	[5x] zu Hohn und Jammer
I am condemned.	jagst du mich hin!

SIEGFRIED
(leaps down from the rock and approaches.) [68x, 18]

The night draws on:	Die Nacht bricht an:
and there in your cave	[71] in deinem Gemach
you must obey your husband!	musst du dich mir vermählen!

BRÜNNHILDE

(stretching out threateningly the finger on which she wears Siegfried's ring)

Stand back! See I am guarded!	[5x, 6]	Bleib fern! Fürchte dies Zeichen!
No mortal brings me to shame,		Zur Schande zwingst du mich nicht,
so long as this ring is my guard.	[4y, 18]	solang der Ring mich beschützt.

SIEGFRIED

You shall be conquered by Gunther;	[68x, 5x]	Mannesrecht gebe er Gunther,
and that ring makes you his wife!		durch den Ring sei ihm vermählt!

BRÜNNHILDE

Stand back, and fear me!		Zurück, du Räuber!
Foolhardy thief!		Frevelnder Dieb!
Beware me, I'm armed by the ring!	[6, 5b]	Erfreche dich nicht, mir zu nahn!
Stronger than steel		Stärker als Stahl
makes me the ring:		macht mich der Ring:
No! None steals from me!	[34]	nie — raubst du ihn mir!

SIEGFRIED

From you I shall take it,	[23]	Von dir ihn zu lösen,
taught by your words!		lehrst du mich nun!

(He pulls her towards him. They struggle. [78, 5x, 34] Brünnhilde wrenches herself free, runs away and turns as if to defend herself. [66] Siegfried seizes her again. She escapes; he catches her. They wrestle furiously. He seizes her by the hand and draws the ring from her finger. Brünnhilde shrieks violently. [23, 34, 72] As she sinks down into his arms, as if broken, her unconscious look meets Siegfried's eyes [65]. He lets her fainting body sink to the stone bench at the entrance to the cave. [18])

Now you are mine.	[71]	Jetzt bist du mein,
Brünnhilde, Gunther's bride,		Brünnhilde, Gunthers Braut —
there we shall stay in your cave!		Gönne mir nun dein Gemach!

BRÜNNHILDE

(stares before her, fainting, exhausted) [22]

Now nothing can save me,	[65]	Was könntest du wehren,
ill-fated wife!		elendes Weib?

Siegfried drives her on with a gesture of command. Trembling, and with faltering steps, she goes into the cave. [68x, 22, 78, 5x]

SIEGFRIED

(draws his sword; in his natural voice:) [79, 27, 9a]

Now, Notung, witness here	[76a, 74]	Nun, Notung, zeuge du,
how I shall keep my vow.		dass ich in Züchten warb.
I keep my word to my brother!	[75,76c]	Die Treue wahrend dem Bruder,
Part me now from Gunther's bride!	[27, 79]	trenne mich von seiner Braut!

He follows Brünnhilde. [18, 71, 65, 79]

The curtain falls.

Act Two

An open space on the shore. In front of the Gibichung hall: on the right, the open entrance to the hall; on the left, the bank of the Rhine, from which, slanting across the stage to the back at the right, rises a rocky height cut by several mountain paths. There Fricka's altar-stone is visible; higher up is a larger one for Wotan and, on the side, a similar one dedicated to Donner. It is night.

Scene One. *Hagen, his spear on his arm, his shield at his side, sits sleeping, leaning against one of the doorposts.* [22, 80, 5x, 9a, 68x, 81, 6] *The moon suddenly shines out and throws a bright light on him and his surroundings; Alberich is seen crouching before him, leaning his arms on Hagen's knees.* [6]

ALBERICH
(softly)

Sleep you, Hagen, my son?	[22] Schläfst du, Hagen, mein Sohn?
You sleep, and hear me not;	[76e]Du schläfst und hörst mich nicht,
through sleep I lost my power!	den Ruh' und Schlaf verriet?

HAGEN

(softly, without moving, so that he appears to be sleeping on although his eyes are open) [22, 80x]

I hear you, crafty Niblung;	Ich höre dich, schlimmer Albe:
what have you now to tell my slumber?	was hast du meinem Schlaf zu sagen?

ALBERICH

Remember the power	[5x, 5b, 6]	Gemahnt sei der Macht,
that you were born with,		der du gebietest,
if you've the courage		bist du so mutig,
that your mother gave you at birth!	[7b]	wie die Mutter dich mir gebar!

HAGEN
(as before)

My courage came from her;	[80] Gab mir die Mutter Mut,
no thanks for that I'll grant her,	nicht mag ich ihr doch danken,
for she was bought by your gold.	dass deiner List sie erlag:
Old in youth, gaunt and pale,	frühalt, fahl und bleich,
hating the happy,	hass ich die Frohen,
I'm never glad!	[7b] freue mich nie!

ALBERICH
(as before)

Hagen, my son!	Hagen, mein Sohn!
Cherish that hatred!	Hasse die Frohen!
Then your unhappy,	Mich Lustfreien,
joyless father	Leidbelasteten
you will love as you should!	liebst du so, wie du sollst!
Now be cunning,	Bist du kräftig,
strong and bold!	kühn und klug:
Those whom with weapons	die wir bekämpfen
of darkness we fight,	mit nächtigem Krieg,
soon they shall be destroyed by our hate.	schon gibt ihnen Not unser Neid.
He stole the ring from my hand,	[6] Der einst den Ring mir entriss,
Wotan, that treacherous robber,	Wotan, der wütende Räuber,
but now he has been vanquished	vom eignen Geschlechte
by one of his heroes;	ward er geschlagen:
to the Wälsung he lost	an den Wälsung verlor er
dominion and might;	Macht und Gewalt;
with his band of gods and heroes	[8a] mit der Götter ganzer Sippe
in dread he waits for destruction.	[18] in Angst ersieht er sein Ende.

So I fear him not:
gods and heroes must perish!

Sleep you, Hagen, my son?

Nicht ihn fürcht ich mehr:
fallen muss er mit allen!

Schläfst du, Hagen, mein Sohn?

HAGEN
(*motionless, as before*) [80x]

The might of the gods,
who wins it then?

Der Ewigen Macht,
wer erbte sie?

ALBERICH

I and you!
The world shall be ours,
if I can trust
my scheming son,
if truly you share my hate.
Wotan's spear
was broken by the Wälsung,
and Fafner, the dragon,
was killed by his hand,
and he took the ring as his prize.
Power and might
passed to the Wälsung;
Walhall and Nibelheim
own him as lord.
But that boldest of heroes
is safe from my curse;
for he knows not
the might of the ring;
he makes no use
of its magical power.
Laughter and love fill his heart,
gaily he wastes all his life.
We must destroy him
before we can conquer.

Sleep you, Hagen, my son?

[82] Ich — und du!
Wir erben die Welt.
Trüg ich mich nicht
in deiner Treu',
teilst du meinen Gram und Grimm.
Wotans Speer
[27] zerspellte der Wälsung,
[9a, 52] der Fafner, den Wurm,
im Kampfe gefällt
[6, 13a] und kindisch den Reif sich errang.
Jede Gewalt
hat er gewonnen;
Walhall und Nibelheim
neigen sich ihm.
An dem furchtlosen Helden
erlahmt selbst mein Fluch:
denn nicht kennt er
des Ringes Wert,
zu nichts nützt er
die neidlichste Macht.
[45] Lachend in liebender Brunst,
brennt er lebend dahin.
[68x] Ihn zu verderben,
[7b] taugt uns nun einzig!

Schläfst du, Hagen, mein Sohn?

HAGEN
(*as before*) [22]

Towards his destruction
Siegfried is bound.

Zu seinem Verderben
dient er mir schon.

ALBERICH

The golden ring,
that ring — you have to win it!
For he is loved
by a woman who is wise;
if she advise
that he return it,
if the Rhine's fair maids,
whom once I pursued,
by chance recover the ring,
we've lost it; gone is our gold,
and no craft can win it again.
Wake from your slumber,
strive for the ring!
For fearless and bold
you were bred,
so that you'd fight my foes
when I needed.
Though you were too weak
to fight with the giant,
whom only Siegfried could slay,

[82] Den golden Ring,
den Reif gilt's zu erringen!
[41] Ein weises Weib
lebt dem Wälsung zulieb:
[5x] riet es ihn je
des Rheines Töchtern,
[2] die in Wassers Tiefen
einst mich betört,
[6] zurückzugeben den Ring,
verloren ging' mir das Gold,
keine List erlangte es je.
[82] Drum ohne Zögern
ziel auf den Reif!
[12] Dich Zaglosen
zeugt' ich mir ja,
dass wider Helden
hart du mir hieltest.
[52] Zwar stark nicht genug,
den Wurm zu bestehn,
[46] was allein dem Wälsung bestimmt,

yet deadly hatred	[82]	zu zähem Hass doch
I bred in Hagen		erzog ich Hagen,
so he could avenge me;		der soll mich nun rächen,
the ring he'll win me,	[7b]	den Ring gewinnen
though Wälsung and Wotan conspire!		dem Wälsung und Wotan zum Hohn!
Swear to me, Hagen, my son!	[8]	Schwörst du mir's, Hagen, mein Sohn?

From this point a gradually darkening shadow again covers Alberich. At the same time, day begins to dawn.

HAGEN
(still as before) [22, 80]

| That ring shall be Hagen's; | | Den Ring soll ich haben: |
| leave me in peace! | | harre in Ruh'! |

ALBERICH

| Swear to me, Hagen, my son! | | Schwörst du mir's, Hagen, mein Held? |

HAGEN

| To myself I swear it; | [80] | Mir selbst schwör ich's; |
| trust me, and fear not! | [23] | schweige die Sorge! |

ALBERICH
(gradually disappearing from sight, while his voice becomes ever less audible)

Be true, Hagen, my son!		Sei treu, Hagen, mein Sohn!
Crafty hero! Be true!		Trauter Helde! — Sei treu!
Be true! True!	[5x]	Sei treu! — Treu!

Alberich has entirely disappeared. Hagen, who has remained in the same position, gazes motionless and with fixed eyes towards the Rhine, over which the light of dawn is spreading. The Rhine begins to glow more and more brightly with the red light of dawn. [83, 4x]

Scene Two. *Hagen starts violently* [83x, 18]. *Siegfried appears suddenly from behind a bush close to the shore. He appears in his own shape but still has the Tarnhelm on his head. He takes it off and hangs it from his belt as he comes forward.*

SIEGFRIED

Hoiho! Hagen!	[45]	Hoiho, Hagen!
Fast asleep?		Müder Mann!
Did I surprise you?		Siehst du mich kommen?

HAGEN
(rising leisurely)

Hi, Siegfried!	[83]	Hei, Siegfried!
You're back so early!		Geschwinder Helde!
Where have you been?		Wo brausest du her?

SIEGFRIED

At Brünnhilde's rock!	[13a]	Vom Brünnhildenstein!
And there I drew the breath		Dort sog ich den Atem ein,
with which I just called:		mit dem ich dich rief:
the Tarnhelm carried me fast.	[45]	so schnell war meine Fahrt!
Slowly there follow a pair;	[34]	Langsamer folgt mir ein Paar:
by boat they will arrive!		zu Schiff gelangt das her!

HAGEN

| You conquered Brünnhild? | | So zwangst du Brünnhild? |

SIEGFRIED

| Where's Gutrune? | | Wacht Gutrune? |

HAGEN
(calling towards the hall)

| Hoiho, Gutrune! | [73] | Hoiho, Gutrune, |
| Join us here! | | komm heraus! |

Siegfried is back;
come, welcome him.

[13a] Siegfried ist da:
was säumst du drin?

SIEGFRIED
(*turning to the hall*)

I'll tell you both
how I won Brünnhild's hand.

Euch beiden meld ich,
wie ich Brünnhild band.

(*Gutrune comes from the hall to meet him.*) [73]

Now make me welcome,
Gibich maid!
I bring the news you long to hear.

[73b] Heiss mich wilkommen,
Gibichskind!
Ein guter Bote bin ich dir.

GUTRUNE

May Freia smile on you
in the name of all lovely women!

[73] Freia grüsse dich
[73b]zu aller Frauen Ehre!

SIEGFRIED

One alone
is all I care for!
As wife, I win you today.

Frei und hold
sei nun mir Frohem:
zum Weib gewann ich dich heut.

GUTRUNE

And so Brünnhild's with my brother?

So folgt Brünnhild meinem Bruder?

SIEGFRIED

Soon she was won as his bride.

Leicht ward die Frau ihm gefreit.

GUTRUNE

Was he unharmed by the fire?

Sengte das Feuer ihn nicht?

SIEGFRIED

He could have passed through the flame,
but in his place I went instead,
for thus I planned to win you.

Ihn hätt' es auch nicht versehrt,
doch ich durchschritt es für ihn,
[73] da dich ich wollt' erwerben.

GUTRUNE

And you? You were not hurt?

Doch dich hat es verschont?

SIEGFRIED

I laughed at the threat of the flames.

Mich freute die schwebende Brunst.

GUTRUNE

Did Brünnhild think you were Gunther? [13a]Hielt Brünnhild dich für Gunther?

SIEGFRIED

No one could tell us apart;
the Tarnhelm served me well,
as Hagen told me it would.

Ihm glich ich auf das Haar;
[18] der Tarnhelm wirkte das,
wie Hagen tüchtig es wies.

HAGEN

I gave you good advice.

Dir gab ich guten Rat.

GUTRUNE

You mastered that fearless maid?

So zwangst du das kühne Weib?

SIEGFRIED

She felt — Gunther's force.

[69] Sie wich — Gunthers Kraft.

GUTRUNE

But she gave herself to you?

[34, 5x] Und vermählte sie sich dir?

SIEGFRIED

Through the night the dauntless Brünnhild
did obey her husband and lord.

Ihrem Mann gehorchte Brünnhild
eine volle bräutliche Nacht.

GUTRUNE

But that husband was really you?   [71] Als ihr Mann doch galtest du?

SIEGFRIED

To Gutrune I was faithful.   [73] Bei Gutrune weilte Siegfried.

GUTRUNE

Yet my Siegfried was with Brünnhild?   [34, 5x] Doch zur Seite war ihm Brünnhild?

SIEGFRIED
(pointing to his sword)

Between the east and west lies north: [79, 27, 9a] Zwischen Ost und West der Nord:
so near was Brünnhild — yet so far.   [76a] so nah — war Brünnhild ihm fern.

GUTRUNE

Then how did Gunther obtain his bride?   Wie empfing Gunther sie nun von dir?

SIEGFRIED

When the dawn came, the firelight was   Durch des Feuers verlöschende Lohe
   fading,
the mists fell as she followed me   [13a] im Frühnebel vom Felsen
down to the vale below;   folgte sie mir zu Tal;
   and by the shore   [34]   dem Strande nah,
there we changed   flugs die Stelle
our places, Gunther and I;   tauschte Gunther mit mir;
and by the magic Tarnhelm   durch des Geschmeides Tugend
I returned back here to you.   wünscht' ich mich schnell hierher.
The wind is fair, and soon   [45, 83] Ein starker Wind nun treibt
the lovers will reach the shore.   die Trauten den Rhein herauf:
Let us welcome them when they come.   [73] drum rüstet jetzt den Empfang!

GUTRUNE

Siegfried! Mightiest of men!   Siegfried, mächtigster Mann!
I feel strange fear of you!   Wie fasst mich Furcht vor dir!

HAGEN
(looking down the river from a height at the back)

I can see a sail in the distance.   [73] In der Ferne seh ich ein Segel.

SIEGFRIED

Then give the herald thanks!   So sagt dem Boten Dank!

GUTRUNE

Let us prepare a splendid welcome,   [73b] Lasset uns sie hold empfangen,
and make her glad to stay among us.   dass heiter sie und gern hier weile!
   You, Hagen,   [73]   Du, Hagen, minnig
   call the vassals together,   rufe die Mannen
in Gibich's hall we'll feast them!   [73b] nach Gibichs Hof zur Hochzeit!
   Lovely women   [75]   Frohe Frauen
   I'll bring with me.   ruf ich zum Fest:
They'll join us here, share in our joy.   der Freudigen folgen sie gern.
     (As she goes towards the hall, she turns round again.) [73]
Siegfried, will you rest?   Rastest du, schlimmer Held?

SIEGFRIED

Helping Gutrun gives me rest.   Dir zu helfen, ruh ich aus.

     He gives her his hand and goes into the hall with her.

Scene Three.

HAGEN
(Having mounted a rock high at the back of the stage, he places his cowhorn to his lips and sounds it, turning to the countryside.)]83]

Hoiho! Hoihohoho!   [5x] Hoiho! Hoihohoho!

You Gibich vassals,		Ihr Gibichsmannen,
answer my call.		machet euch auf!
Waken! Waken!	[83x, 5x]	Wehe! Wehe!
Hear me! Hear me!		Waffen! Waffen!
Arm all our land!	[73]	Waffen durchs Land!
Bring your weapons!		Gute Waffen!
Mighty weapons!		Starke Waffen!
Sharp and bright!	[69]	Scharf zum Streit!
Foes are here!	[25]	Not ist da!
Foes! Waken! Waken!		Not! Wehe! Wehe!
Hoiho! Hoihohoho!	[83x]	Hoiho! Hoihohoho!

Hagen remains in the same position on the rock. He blows his horn again. Other horns answer from different parts of the countryside. By different paths, armed vassals rush on first singly, then in increasing numbers, assembling on the shore in front of the hall.

THE VASSALS
(first singly, then joined by the newcomers)

I hear the horn!	[84]	Was tost das Horn?
Who sounds the alarm?		Was ruft es zu Heer?
We come with our arms!		Wir kommen mit Wehr,
We come with our weapons!		wir kommen mit Waffen!
Hagen! Hagen!		Hagen! Hagen!
Hoiho! Hoiho!		Hoiho! Hoiho!
What's the danger here?		Welche Not ist da?
Say what foe is near!		Welcher Feind ist nah?
Who comes to fight?		Wer gibt uns Streit?
Is Gunther in need?	[69]	Ist Gunther in Not?
We come with our weapons,		Wir kommen mit Waffen,
with weapons of might.		mit scharfer Wehr.
Hoiho! Ho! Hagen!		Hoiho! Ho! Hagen!

HAGEN
(still from the height) [73]

Come to my call,		Rüstet euch wohl
and arm yourselves!		und rastet nicht;
Gunther soon shall return:		Gunther sollt ihr empfahn:
his wife joins us today!		ein Weib hat der gefreit.

THE VASSALS

| What is his need? | [84] | Drohet ihm Not? |
| Who is his foe? | | Drängt ihn der Feind? |

HAGEN

| His proud, fiery wife | | Ein freisliches Weib |
| joins us today. | | führet er heim. |

THE VASSALS

| And is he pursued | | Ihm folgen der Magen |
| by furious kinsmen? | | feindliche Mannen? |

HAGEN

| No one follows them; | [7b] | Einsam fährt er: |
| they are alone. | | keiner folgt. |

THE VASSALS

Then his danger is past?		So bestand er die Not?
And his fight has been won?		So bestand er den Kampf?
Tell us all!		Sag es an!

HAGEN

The hero has gained him	[45]	Der Wurmtöter
a bride;		wehrte der Not:
Siegfried, his friend,		Siegfried, der Held,
saved him from harm!		der schuf ihm Heil!

95

Then why have you called us together?　[84]　Was soll ihm das Heer nun noch helfen?

TEN OTHERS

Then why have we been called?　　　　Was hilft ihm nun das Heer?

HAGEN

Sacred oxen　　　　　　　　　　　Starke Stiere
must be slaughtered;　　　　　　　sollt ihr schlachten;
on Wotan's altar　　　　[83]　　　am Weihstein fliesse
pour forth their blood!　　　　　　Wotan ihr Blut!

ONE VASSAL

Then, Hagen, what would you have us do?　Was, Hagen, was heissest du uns dann?

EIGHT VASSALS

What would you have us do?　　　　Was heissest du uns dann?

FOUR OTHERS

What should we do?　　　　　　　Was soll es dann?

ALL

What would you have us do?　　　　Was heissest du uns dann?

HAGEN

Take a boar as offering,　　　　　Einen Eber fällen
kill it for Froh;　　　　　　　　sollt ihr für Froh!
and a goat in its prime　　　　　Einen stämmigen Bock
strike down for Donner!　　　　　stechen für Donner!
Sheep should then　　　　　　　Schafe aber
be slaughtered for Fricka,　　　　schlachtet für Fricka,
and then she will smile on this wedding!　dass gute Ehe sie gebe!

THE VASSALS
(*with ever-increasing hilarity*)

After these offerings,　　　　　　Schlugen wir Tiere,
what next should we do?　　　　　was schaffen wir dann?

HAGEN

Your drinkhorns take,　　　　　　Das Trinkhorn nehmt,
and ask your women　　　[83]　　von trauten Fraun
to fill with wine　　　　　　　　mit Met und Wein
until they run full!　　　　　　　wonnig gefüllt!

THE VASSALS

Our drinkhorns in hand　　[84]　　Das Trinkhorn zur Hand,
what ought we then to do?　　　　wie halten wir es dann?

HAGEN

Seize them, and drink　　　　　　Rüstig gezecht,
till you can drink no more!　　　　bis der Rausch euch zähmt!
So shall our gods be honoured,　　Alles den Göttern zu Ehren,
and they will grant us their blessing!　dass gute Ehe sie geben!

THE VASSALS
(*break into ringing laughter.*) [83x]

Glad times have come,　　[83]　　Gross Glück und Heil
come to our Rhine,　　　　　　　lacht nun dem Rhein,
when Hagen, grim Hagen,　　　　da Hagen, der Grimme,
with laughter can shine!　　　　　so lustig mag sein!
Our hedge's thorn　　　　　　　Der Hagedorn
pricks us no more;　　　　　　　sticht nun nicht mehr;
our bridal herald　　　　[73]　　zum Hochzeitsrufer
calls us to wine!　　　　　　　　ward er bestellt.

HAGEN

(who has remained very serious, has come down to the vassals and now stands among them.) [84]

Now stop your laughter,	Nun lasst das Lachen,
faithful vassals!	mut' ge Mannen!
Receive Gunther's bride!	Empfangt Gunthers Braut!
Brünnhilde soon shall be here.	Brünnhilde naht dort mit ihm.

(He points towards the Rhine. Some of the vassals run to the height, while others take up a position on the shore to see the arrival. Hagen approaches some of the vassals.) [73]

Honour your lady,		Hold seid der Herrin,
come to her aid;		helfet ihr treu:
if she is wronged,	[68x]	traf sie ein Leid,
you must revenge her!		rasch seid zur Rache!

He turns slowly aside towards the back. During the following chorus, the boat with Gunther and Brünnhilde appears on the Rhine. [73, 83x]

THE VASSALS
(first singly, then more, then all)

Hail! Hail!	Heil! Heil!
Be welcome! Be welcome!	Willkommen! Willkommen!

(Some vassals leap into the river and draw the boat to the shore. All press closer to the bank.)

Be welcome, Gunther!	Willkommen! Gunther!
Hail! Hail!	Heil! Heil!

Scene Four. *Gunther steps out of the boat with Brünnhilde: the vassals range themselves respectfully to receive them. During the following, Gunther ceremoniously leads Brünnhilde forward by the hand.*

THE VASSALS

Welcome, Gunther!	Heil dir, Gunther!
Hail to you, and to your bride!	Heil dir und deiner Braut!
Hail! Hail!	Willkommen!

They clash their weapons noisily together.

GUNTHER
(presenting Brünnhilde, who follows him with pale face and downcast eyes, to the vassals)
[34]

Brünnhild, my fairest bride,	Brünnhild, die hehrste Frau,
joins us beside the Rhine.	bring ich euch her zum Rhein.
And no man could win	Ein edleres Weib
a nobler woman.	ward nie gewonnen.
The Gibichungs have been blessed;	Der Gibichungen Geschlecht,
gods show their grace once again.	gaben die Götter ihm Gunst,
To new renown	zum höchsten Ruhm
we rise today!	rag' es nun auf!

THE VASSALS
(clashing their weapons)

Hail, lord,	Heil dir,
glorious Gibichung!	glücklicher Gibichung!

Gunther leads Brünnhilde, who has never raised her eyes, to the hall, from which Siegfried and Gutrune now come forth, attended by women. [34, 78, 73]

GUNTHER
(stops before the hall.)

I greet you, noble friend,		Gegrüsst sei, teurer Held;
and you, lovely sister!		gegrüsst, holde Schwester!
Gladly I see you beside him,	[74]	Dich seh ich froh ihm zur Seite,
my friend who won you for wife.		der dich zum Weib gewann.
Two pairs in wedlock		Zwei sel'ge Paare
here shall find blessing.		seh ich hier prangen:

(He draws Brünnhilde forwards.) [73]

Brünnhild — and Gunther,	Brünnhild — und Gunther,
Gutrun — and Siegfried!	Gutrun – und Siegfried!

97

Brünnhilde, startled, raises her eyes and sees Siegfried; her look remains fixed on him in amazement. [6, 46] *Gunther, who has released Brünnhilde's violently trembling hand, shows, as do all, blank astonishment at Brünnhilde's behaviour.* [78]

SOME VASSALS

What ails her? Is she distraught? [38, 18] Was ist ihr? Ist sie entrückt?

Brünnhilde begins to tremble.

SIEGFRIED
(taking a few steps towards Brünnhilde) [71]

What clouds Brünnhilde's brow? Was müht Brünnhildes Blick?

BRÜNNHILDE
(scarcely able to control herself) [73]

Siegfried ... here ... ! Gutrune ... ? Siegfried ... hier ... ! Gutrune ... ?

SIEGFRIED

Gunther's gentle sister, Gunthers milde Schwester:
  won by me,   mir vermählt
  as, by Gunther, you.   wie Gunther du.

BRÜNNHILDE
(with terrible violence)

I ... Gunther ... ? You lie! Ich ... Gunther ... ? Du lügst!
(She appears to be about to fall. Siegfried, beside her, supports her.) [38]
My eyes grow dim ... Mir schwindet das Licht ...
     (In Siegfried's arms, she looks up faintly at his face.) [65]
Siegfried — knows me not? Siegfried — kennt mich nicht?

SIEGFRIED

Gunther, your wife is troubled! Gunther, deinem Weib ist übel!
     (Gunther comes to them.)
Arouse yourself! Erwache, Frau!
Here stands your husband. Hier steht dein Gatte.

BRÜNNHILDE
(sees the ring on Siegfried's outstretched finger, and starts with terrible violence.) [6]

Ha! — The ring ... Ha! — der Ring ...
upon his hand! an seiner Hand!
He ... Siegfried? [23] Er ... Siegfried?

SOME VASSALS

What's this? What's this? Was ist? Was ist?

HAGEN
(advancing among the vassals, from the back)

Now mark her words, Jetzt merket klug,
let her charge be heard! was die Frau euch klagt!

BRÜNNHILDE
(tries to recover herself, while she forcibly restrains the most terrible excitement.) [22]

A ring I see Einen Ring sah ich
upon your hand; an deiner Hand.
that ring was stolen, Nicht dir gehört er,
it was taken — ihn entriss mir
     (pointing to Gunther)
— seized by him! — dieser Mann!
So how did you gain Wie mochtest von ihm
that ring from his hand? den Ring du empfahn?

SIEGFRIED
(attentively observes the ring on his finger.)

This ring? Den Ring empfing ich
I had it not from him. [71, 3] nicht von ihm.

BRÜNNHILDE
(to Gunther)

If you did steal my ring,	[5x, 5b] Nahmst du von mir den Ring,
when I became your bride,	durch den ich dir vermählt;
then claim it as your right,	so melde ihm dein Recht,
make him return the ring!	fordre zurück das Pfand!

GUNTHER
(in great perplexity)

The ring? I gave him nothing:	[71] Den Ring? Ich gab ihm keinen:
yet — are you sure it is yours?	doch — kennst du ihn auch gut?

BRÜNNHILDE

What did you do with the ring,	Wo bärgest du den Ring,
when from my hand you stole it?	[3] den du von mir erbeutet?
(Gunther, greatly confused, is silent. [18] *She breaks out in violent passion.)* [78]	
Ha! — Siegfried stole it;	Ha! — Dieser war es,
he took the ring from me:	der mir den Ring entriss:
Siegfried, a traitor and thief!	[6] Siegfried, der trugvolle Dieb!

All look expectantly at Siegfried, who is absorbed in distant thoughts while contemplating the ring. [78, 6]

SIEGFRIED

No woman's hand	Von keinem Weib
gave me the ring,	kam mir der Reif;
nor was it stolen	[21] noch war's ein Weib,
from any woman's hand:	dem ich ihn abgewann:
I know full well	genau erkenn ich
where I found this ring,	[4] des Kampfes Lohn,
for at Neidhöhl I won it myself,	den vor Neidhöhl' einst ich bestand,
when I fought with Fafner the giant.	[3] als den starken Wurm ich erschlug.

HAGEN
(coming between them)

Brünnhild, are you sure	Brünnhild', kühne Frau,
you recognise the ring?	[3] kennst du genau den Ring?
For if it is Gunther's ring,	Ist's der, den du Gunther gabst,
if it is his,	[68x] so ist er sein,
then Siegfried was false to his friend;	[39] und Siegfried gewann ihn durch Trug,
he must pay then for his treachery!	[71] den der Treulose büssen sollt'!

BRÜNNHILDE
(crying out in most terrible anguish)

Betrayed! Betrayed!	[5x] Betrug! Betrug!
Shamefully betrayed!	[6] Schändlichster Betrug!
Deceit! Deceit!	[5x] Verrat! Verrat!
How can I be revenged?	[78] Wie noch nie er gerächt!

GUTRUNE

Betrayed? By whom?	Verrat? An wem?

VASSALS AND WOMEN

Betrayed? By whom?	[78] Verrat? An wem?

BRÜNNHILDE

Hear in Walhall,	[8] Heil'ge Götter,
mighty immortals!	himmlische Lenker!
Have you ordained	[78] Rauntet ihr dies
this dark decree?	[22] in eurem Rat?
Why have you doomed me	Lehrt ihr mich Leiden,
to anguish and grief?	wie keiner sie litt?
Why have you plunged me	Schuft ihr mir Schmach,
in sadness and shame?	wie nie sie geschmerzt?
Teach me a vengeance	[6] Ratet nun Rache,

more cruel than my grief!
Stir me to rage
still more keen than my shame!
Ah, though Brünnhilde's
heart may be broken,
bring her betrayer
soon to his death!

wie nie sie gerast!
Zündet mir Zorn,
wie noch nie er gezähmt!
[42] Heisset Brünnhild,
ihr Herz zu zerbrechen,
den zu zertrümmern,
der sie betrog!

GUNTHER

Brünnhild, beloved!
Calm yourself!

[84] Brünnhild, Gemahlin!
Mäss'ge dich!

BRÜNNHILDE

Away, betrayer,
self-betrayed one!
All of you, hear me:
not he
but — Siegfried there
made me his wife.

[78] Weich fern, Verräter!
Selbst Verratner!
Wisset denn alle:
nicht ihm —
dem Manne dort
bin ich vermählt.

WOMEN

Siegfried? Gutrune's husband?

Siegfried? Gutruns Gemahl?

VASSALS

Gutrune's husband?

Gutruns Gemahl?

BRÜNNHILDE

He forced delight
and love from me.

[7b] Er zwang mir Lust
und Liebe ab.

SIEGFRIED

Can you defile
your fame so lightly?
Then hear me — I'll defend it,
for I accuse you of falsehood!
Hear how I kept my word!
Blood brotherhood
I and Gunther had sworn:
Notung, my faithful sword,
guarded that holy vow:
this shining blade divided me
from this unhappy wife.

[78] Achtest du so
der eignen Ehre?
Die Zunge, die sie lästert,
muss ich der Lüge sie zeihen?
Hört, ob ich Treue brach!
[68x, 76a] Blutbrüderschaft
[79] hab ich Gunther geschworen:
[27, 9a] Notung, das werte Schwert,
wahrte der Treue Eid;
[78] mich trennte seine Schärfe
von diesem traur'gen Weib.

BRÜNNHILDE

You crafty man,
hear how you lie!
Calling on the sword
which shared in your shame!
I know its shining sharpness;
I know too the scabbard
in which it slept
all night on the wall —
Notung, that trusty sword —
while its master was faithless to his word.

Du listiger Held,
sieh, wie du lügst!
Wie auf dein Schwert
du schlecht dich berufst!
[27] Wohl kenn ich seine Schärfe,
[66] doch kenn auch die Scheide,
darin so wonnig
ruht' an der Wand
Notung, der treue Freund,
als die Traute sein Herr sich gewann.

THE VASSALS
(gathering indignantly) [84]

Was Siegfried a traitor,
tarnishing Gunther's honour?

Wie? Brach er die Treue?
Trübte er Gunthers Ehre?

THE WOMEN

Siegfried a traitor?

[66] Brach er die Treue?

100

The oath on the spear, Act Two at Bayreuth: the 1974 Wolfgang Wagner production (above) and (below) the Peter Hall production, 1984 (photos: Festspielleitung Bayreuth)

GUNTHER
(to Siegfried)

My name's dishonoured,	[5x]	Geschändet wär' ich,
stained with disgrace,		schmählich bewahrt,
unless you deny it;		gäbst du die Rede
swear that she lies!		nicht ihr zurück!

GUTRUNE

Faithless Siegfried,	[66, 5x]	Treulos, Siegfried,
false to your vow?		sännest du Trug?
Assure me that all		Bezeuge, dass jene
she says is a lie!		falsch dich zeiht!

THE VASSALS

Answer the charge,		Reinige dich,
if you are true!		bist du im Recht!
Swear on a spear-point!		Schweige die Klage!
Swear with a vow!		Schwöre den Eid!

SIEGFRIED

I shall answer		Schweig' ich die Klage,
swearing a vow:		schwör' ich den Eid:
which of you warriors		wer von euch wagt
will lend me his spear?		seine Waffe daran?

HAGEN

Let my spear-point serve you!	[68x, 78]	Meines Speeres Spitze
Swear on the spear:		wag ich daran:
my spear shall witness your vow!		sie wahr' in Ehren den Eid.

The vassals form a ring round Siegfried and Hagen. Hagen holds out his spear: Siegfried lays two fingers of his right hand upon the spear-point. [76e, 76c, 78]

SIEGFRIED

Shining steel!	[85]	Helle Wehr!
Holiest weapon!	[68x]	Heilige Waffe!
Help me defend my honour!	[73x, 78]	Hilf meinem ewigen Eide!
On this shining spear-point		Bei des Speeres Spitze
sworn is my vow:		sprech ich den Eid:
spear-point, witness my word!		Spitze, achte des Spruchs!
If I acted falsely,	[82]	Wo Scharfes mich schneidet,
strike at my heart;		schneide du mich;
when my death comes to claim me,		wo der Tod mich soll treffen,
yours be the stroke:		treffe du mich:
if what she says is true,		klagte das Weib dort wahr,
if I my brother betrayed!		brach ich dem Bruder den Eid!

BRÜNNHILDE

(She strides angrily into the circle, tears Siegfried's hand away from the spear and seizes the point with her own hand.) [34, 35, 66]

Shining steel!	[85]	Helle Wehr!
Holiest weapon!	[68x]	Heilige Waffe!
Help me defend my honour!		Hilf meinem ewigen Eide!
On this shining spear-point	[78]	Bei des Speeres Spitze
sworn is my vow:		sprech ich den Eid:
spear-point, witness my word!		Spitze, achte des Spruchs!
Devote your mighty strength	[82]	Ich weihe deine Wucht,
to his destruction!	[27b, 68x, 78]	dass sie ihn werfe!
For his treachery he must die,		Deine Schärfe segne ich,
strike him and kill him!		dass sie ihn schneide:
For he has betrayed every vow,		denn, brach seine Eide er all,
and falsehood now he has sworn!		schwur Meineid jetzt dieser Mann!

(in wild excitement) [13b]

Help, Donner!	Hilf, Donner,
Send us your thunder,	tose dein Wetter,
to silence this shameful disgrace!	[66] zu schweigen die wütende Schmach!

SIEGFRIED

Gunther, look to your wife there;	Gunther, wehr deinem Weibe,
she dares to slander your name.	das schamlos Schande dir lügt!
Grant her time and rest,	[5x, 78] Gönnt ihr Weil' und Ruh'
this furious mountain maid,	der wilden Felsenfrau,
until her frenzied rage is over;	[30b] dass ihre freche Wut sich lege,
I fear some demon's	die eines Unholds
evil spell	arge List
makes her so fierce with us all!	wider uns alle erregt!
You vassals, leave her alone!	Ihr Mannen, kehret euch ab!
Leave this woman to scold!	Lasst das Weibergekeif!
Like cowards, men quit the field	[19] Als Zage weichen wir gern,
when it's a battle of words.	gilt es mit Zungen den Streit.

(He comes close to Gunther.) [27a, 13a]

Friend, it grieves me more than you	Glaub, mehr zürnt es mich als dich,
that my deception failed:	dass schlecht ich sie getäuscht:
the Tarnhelm, I suspect,	[18] der Tarnhelm, dünkt mich fast,
was not a full disguise.	hat halb mich nur gehehlt.
But woman's rage	[6] Doch Frauengroll
is soon at an end:	friedet sich bald:
she will soon learn to love you;	dass ich dir es gewann,
then she will thank me as well.	[66] dankt dir gewiss noch das Weib.

(He turns again to the vassals.)

Follow, you vassals!	[84] Munter, ihr Mannen!
On to the feast!	Folgt mir zum Mahl!

(to the women) [73]

Come, fair women,	Froh zur Hochzeit
help at our wedding!	helfet, ihr Frauen!
Share my delight,	Wonnige Lust
laugh at my joy!	lach nun auf!
In house and field,	In Hof und Hain,
carefree and merry	heiter vor allen
you shall find me today.	sollt ihr heute mich sehn,
When by love I am blessed,	[76] Wen die Minne freut,
I want only laughter;	meinem frohen Mute
all of you share in my joy!	tu es der Glückliche gleich!

In exuberant happiness, he throws his arm round Gutrune and leads her away with him into the hall. The vassals and the women, carried away by his example, follow him. [73] Only Brünnhilde, Gunther and Hagen remain behind. Gunther, his face covered, has seated himself on one side in abject despair. Brünnhilde, standing in the foreground, gazes sorrowfully after Siegfried and Gutrune for a while, and then droops her head in thought.
[23, 7b, 66, 80, 76e, 22, 82]

Scene Five.

BRÜNNHILDE
(engrossed in contemplation) [78]

Dark, unholy powers	Welches Unholds List
lie here around me!	liegt hier verhohlen?
Dark, enchanted spells	Welches Zaubers Rat
spun for my doom!	regte dies auf?
What use is my wisdom	[38] Wo ist nun mein Wissen
against this witchcraft?	gegen dies Wirrsal?
What use is my reason	Wo sind meine Runen
to solve these riddles?	gegen dies Rätsel?
Oh sorrow! Sorrow!	Ach Jammer, Jammer!
Grief and sorrow!	Weh, ach Wehe!

All my wisdom
I gave to him!
And I remain
held by his might;
and now he holds me here
as his hostage,
shamed, helpless; and in my shame
gladly he gives me away!

Whose hand can help me now?
Whose sword can sever my bonds?

[56] All mein Wissen
wies ich ihm zu!
[66] In seiner Macht
hält er die Magd;
in seinen Banden
hält er die Beute,
die, jammernd ob ihrer Schmach,
[82] jauchzend der Reiche verschenkt!

[5x, 78] Wer bietet mir nun das Schwert,
mit dem ich die Bande zerschnitt'?

HAGEN
(*coming close to Brünnhilde*) [85]

Have trust in me,
offended wife!
I can revenge
such treachery.

Vertraue mir,
betrogne Frau!
Wer dich verriet,
das räche ich.

BRÜNNHILDE
(*looking round wearily*)

On whom?

An wem?

HAGEN

On Siegfried, he who was false.

An Siegfried, der dich betrog.

BRÜNNHILDE

On Siegfried? ... You?

An Siegfried? ... du?
(*smiling bitterly*)

One single flash
from the eyes of the hero,
even veiled by the Tarnhelm's disguise,
such as lighted on me,
and the bravest foe
cringes with terror!

Ein einz'ger Blick
seines blitzenden Auges,
[71] das selbst durch die Lügenstalt
leuchtend strahlte zu mir,
[45] deinen besten Mut
machte er bangen!

HAGEN

But on my spear-point
he swore his falsehood!

[85] Doch meinem Speere
spart' ihn sein Meineid?

BRÜNNHILDE

Truth and falsehood,
what do they mean!
With stronger spells
you must arm your spear-point,
if you would strike at his strength!

Eid und Meineid,
müssige Acht!
[39] Nach Stärkrem späh,
deinen Speer zu waffnen,
willst du den Stärksten bestehn!

HAGEN

I know of Siegfried's
conquering might,
and of his strength in a battle;
so whisper to me
some crafty means
to make him fall to my spear.

[82] Wohl kenn ich Siegfrieds
siegende Kraft,
wie schwer im Kampf er zu fällen;
drum raune nun du
mir guten Rat,
wie doch der Recke mir wich'?

BRÜNNHILDE

Ungrateful, shameful return!
By magic arts
I wove a spell,
to protect his life from his foes!
My charms surround him
and guard his life;
my magic keeps him safe from harm.

O Undank, schändlichster Lohn!
Nicht eine Kunst
war mir bekannt,
die zum Heil nicht half seinen Leib!
[58] Unwissend zähmt' ihn
[39] mein Zauberspiel,
das ihn vor Wunden nun gewahrt.

Can no weapon's point then pierce him?   So kann keine Wehr ihm schaden?

BRÜNNHILDE

In battle, none; yet —   Im Kampfe nicht; doch
if at his back you strike ...   [22] träfst du im Rücken ihn ...
    Siegfried, I knew it,   Niemals, das wusst' ich,
he'd never flee,   [39] wich' er dem Feind,
nor turn his back upon his enemy: [27] nie reicht' er fliehend ihm den Rücken:
and there I gave him no blessing.   [58] an ihm drum spart' ich den Segen.

HAGEN

My spear knows where to strike!   [5x, 78] Und dort trifft ihn mein Speer!
        (*He turns quickly from Brünnhilde to Gunther.*)
    Up, Gunther,   Auf, Gunther,
    noble Gibichung!   [76e] edler Gibichung!
Here stands your valiant wife: Hier steht ein starkes Weib;
so why give way to grief?   was hängst du dort in Harm?

GUNTHER
(*starting up passionately*)

    Oh shame!   O Schmach!
    Oh sorrow!   O Schande!
    Woe is me,   Wehe mir,
of all men living the saddest!   [7b] dem jammervollsten Manne!

HAGEN

Your shame overwhelms you;   [78]   In Schande liegst du;
that I grant.   leugn' ich das?

BRÜNNHILDE
(*to Gunther*)

O cowardly man!   O feiger Mann!
Falsest of friends!   falscher Genoss'!
Sheltering behind him,   Hinter dem Helden
scared by the flames,   hehltest du dich,
and then when he'd won me,   dass Preise des Ruhmes
daring to claim me!   [82] er dir erränge!
Deep has sunk   Tief wohl sank
your glorious race,   das teure Geschlecht,
to bear such a coward as you!   das solche Zagen gezeugt!

GUNTHER
(*beside himself*)

Deceived am I — and deceiver!   [78] Betrüger ich – und betrogen!
Betrayed am I — and betrayer!   Verräter ich — und verraten!
So crushed be my bones!   [76e]Zermalmt mir das Mark!
And broken my heart!   Zerbrecht mir die Brust!
Help, Hagen!   [5x] Hilf, Hagen!
And save my honour!   Hilf meiner Ehre!
Help for our mother,   [7b] Hilf deiner Mutter,
for you, too, are her son!   die dich — auch ja gebar!

HAGEN

No hand can help,   [78] Dir hilft kein Hirn,
no deed can atone,   dir hilft keine Hand:
but only — Siegfried's death!   [5x] dir hilft nur — Siegfrieds Tod!

GUNTHER
(*seized with horror*)

Siegfried's death!   Siegfried's Tod?

HAGEN

His death purges your shame!   Nur der sühnt deine Schmach!

105

Siegfried swears on Hagen's spear in Act Two of the Covent Garden production by Götz Friedrich, 1978 (photo: Reg Wilson)

Rita Hunter (left) as Brünnhilde and Elizabeth Connell as Waltraute in the ENO production, designed by Ralph Koltai, 1976 (photo: Reg Wilson)

GUNTHER
(*staring before him*)

Blood-brotherhood	[76b]	Blutbrüderschaft
freely we swore!		schwuren wir uns!

HAGEN

He broke that bond;		Des Bundes Bruch
blood must atone!	[76f]	sühne nun Blut!

GUNTHER

Broke he the bond?	[76e]	Brach er den Bund?

HAGEN

By betraying you!		Da er dich verriet!

GUNTHER

Am I betrayed?		Verriet er mich?

BRÜNNHILDE

He betrayed you;	[76c]	Dich verriet er,
and me — you all have betrayed me!		und mich verrietet ihr alle!
If I had my rights,		Wär' ich gerecht,
all the blood of the world		alles Blut der Welt
could not revenge me for your crime!	[78]	büsste mir nicht eure Schuld!
So the death of one	[82]	Doch des *einen* Tod
now must content me:	[65]	taugt mir für alle:
Siegfried's death		Siegfried falle
atones for his crime, and yours!		zur Sühne für sich und euch!

HAGEN
(*to Gunther, secretly*)

I'll kill him — you shall gain!	[68x]	Er falle — dir zum Heil!
All the world is yours to command	[6]	Ungeheure Macht wird dir,
when you set hands on the ring		gewinnst von ihm du den Ring,
that in death alone he will yield.	[7b]	den der Tod ihm wohl nur entreisst.

GUNTHER
(*softly*)

Brünnhilde's ring?	[66]	Brünnhilde's Ring?

HAGEN

The Nibelung's golden ring.	[5b]	Des Nibelungen Reif.

GUNTHER
(*sighing deeply*)

So Siegfried's doom's decided!	So wär' es Siegfrieds Ende!

HAGEN

His death will serve us all.	[5x, 78]	Uns allen frommt sein Tod.

GUNTHER

Yet Gutrune, ah!	[73]	Doch Gutrune, ach,
Gutrune loves him!		der ich ihn gönnte!
If he should fall at our hands,	[75]	Straften den Gatten wir so,
how can I return to her?		wie bestünden wir vor ihr?

BRÜNNHILDE
(*starting up in a rage*)

What use was my wisdom?		Was riet mir mein Wissen?
What use was my reason?		Was wiesen mich Runen?
In heart-breaking anguish		Im hilflosen Elend
all is revealed:		achtet mir's hell!
Gutrune, she's the enchantress;	[73, 75]	Gutrune heisst der Zauber,
by her spells she stole his love.		der den Gatten mir entzückt!
My curse on her!	[76e]	Angst treffe sie!

Since his death will dismay her,	[72] Muss sein Tod sie betrüben,
we must conceal our deed.	verhehlt sie ihr die Tat.
And so tomorrow	[45] Auf muntres Jagen
when we are hunting,	ziehen wir morgen:
our hero runs on ahead:	der Edle braust uns voran,
we'll find him killed by a boar.	[78, 5x] ein Eber bracht' ihn da um.

GUNTHER AND BRÜNNHILDE

It shall be so!	So soll es sein!
Siegfried dies then!	Siegfried falle!
Freed from the shame	[76e] Sühn' er die Schmach,
cast by his crime!	die er mir schuf!
The vows he swore,	Des Eides Treue
those vows he has broken:	hat er getrogen:
and with his blood	[76f] mit seinem Blut
he shall atone!	büss er die Schuld!
All-guiding	[76e] Allrauner,
god of revenge!	rächender Gott!
All-powerful	Schwurwissender
lord of vows!	Eideshort!
Wotan!	[85] Wotan!
Come to my call!	Wende dich her!
Call up your fearful	Weise die schrecklich
heavenly host;	heilige Schar,
they will obey you;	[82] hieher zu horchen
revenge my wrong!	dem Racheschwur!

HAGEN

Siegfried will die,	[76e] Sterb' er dahin,
destroyed in his pride!	der strahlende Held!
Mine is the ring,	Mein ist der Hort,
my hand soon shall hold it.	mir muss er gehören.
I'll seize that ring;	[76f] Drum sei der Reif
I shall hold it!	ihm entrissen,
Niblung father,	[76e] Alben-Vater,
you fallen lord!	gefallner Fürst!
Night guardian!	Nachthüter!
Nibelung lord!	Niblungenherr!
Alberich!	[68x] Alberich!
Look upon me!	Achte auf mich!
Call once again	Weise von neuem
all your Nibelung host;	der Niblungen Schar,
they will obey you,	[82] dir zu gehorchen,
the ring's true lord!	des Reifes Herrn!

As Gunther turns impetuously with Brünnhilde to the hall, the bridal procession coming out of it meets them. Boys and girls, waving branches of flowers dance happily in front. The men carry Siegfried on a shield and Gutrune on a chair. On the rising ground at the back, by various mountain tracks, serving-men and maids bring sacrificial implements and beasts to the altars, and deck them with flowers. Siegfried and the vassals sound the wedding-call on their horns. [73] The women invite Brünnhilde to accompany them to Gutrune's side. Brünnhilde stares blankly at Gutrune, who beckons her with a friendly smile [75]. As Brünnhilde is about to withdraw impetuously, Hagen steps between them and forces her towards Gunther, who seizes her hand again; he then allows himself to be raised on a shield by the men. [5x, 78] As the procession, scarcely interrupted, quickly starts moving again, towards the height, the curtain falls. [73, 5x, 78]

Act Three

A wild, wooded and rocky valley of the Rhine. [45, 5x, 73, 1a, 4, 3, 86]

Scene One. *The three Rhinemaidens, Woglinde, Wellgunde, and Flosshilde, rise to the surface of the river and swim about, circling as in a dance.* [87, 86]

THE THREE RHINEMAIDENS
(pausing in their swimming)

Fair sunlight	Frau Sonne
shines on us in splendour;	sendet lichte Strahlen;
night lies in the waters;	Nacht liegt in der Tiefe:
they once were bright, [3]	einst war sie hell,
when through the waves	da heil und hehr
our father's gold shone in its splendour!	des Vaters Gold noch in ihr glänzte.
Rhinegold,	Rheingold
shining gold!	klares Gold!
How bright was once your radiance,	Wie hell du einstens strahltest,
noble star of waters!	hehrer Stern der Tiefe!

(They swim about again as in a dance.) [87]

Weialala leia,	Weialala leia,
wallala leialala.	wallala leialala.

(A distant horn-call. They listen. [45] *They joyfully splash the water.)* [86b]

Fair sunlight,	Frau Sonne,
send to us the hero,	sende uns den Helden,
with our gold, which he can give us!	der das Gold uns wiedergäbe!
Then once again, [3]	Liess' er es uns,
when it is returned,	dein lichtes Auge
we shall enjoy its shining splendour!	neideten dann wir nicht länger.
Rhinegold,	Rheingold,
shining gold!	klares Gold!
How fair will be your radiance,	Wie froh du dann strahltest,
noble star of waters!	freier Stern der Tiefe!

Siegfried's horn is heard from the heights. [45]

WOGLINDE

And there is his horn.	Ich höre sein Horn.

WELLGUNDE

The hero's near.	Der Helde naht.

FLOSSHILDE

Let us take counsel!	Lasst uns beraten!

All three dive down quickly. [86] *Siegfried appears on the cliff, fully armed.* [27a]

SIEGFRIED

A goblin led me astray,	Eine Albe führte mich irr,
and now the bear I have lost.	dass ich die Fährte verlor.
You rogue! Have you concealed him?	He, Schelm, in welchem Berge
What have you done with my bear?	bargst du so schnell mir das Wild?

THE THREE RHINEMAIDENS
(rise to the surface again and swim in a ring.)

Siegfried! [87]	Siegfried!

FLOSSHILDE

What makes you grumble and growl?	Was schiltst du so in den Grund?

WELLGUNDE

Has a goblin made you angry?   Welchem Alben bist du gram?

WOGLINDE

Are you annoyed by a gnome?   Hat dich ein Nicker geneckt?

ALL THREE

Tell us, Siegfried, speak to us!   Sag es, Siegfried, sag es uns!

SIEGFRIED
(looking at them with a smile)

Did you entice away   Entzücktet ihr zu euch
that shaggy-coated creature   den zottigen Gesellen,
that I have lost?   der mir verschwand?
Was he your playmate?   Ist's euer Friedel,
If he was your friend,   euch lustigen Frauen
I'll leave him to you.   lass ich ihn gern.

The maidens laugh.

WOGLINDE

Siegfried, if we find your bear,   Siegfried, was gibst du uns,
how will you then reward us?   wenn wir das Wild dir gönnen?

SIEGFRIED

I've had no luck today;   Noch bin ich beutelos;
I've nothing with me to give!   so bittet, was ihr begehrt.

WELLGUNDE

A golden ring   [4x, 3, 6]   Ein goldner Ring
gleams on your finger!   glänzt dir am Finger!

ALL THREE

Come, give it!   Den gib uns!

SIEGFRIED

But to gain this ring   Einen Riesenwurm
I took a dragon's life;   erschlug ich um dem Reif:
to give it for a paltry bear-skin —   für eines schlechten Bären Tatzen
hardly a fair exchange!   böt' ich ihn nun zum Tausch?

WOGLINDE

Are you so mean?   Bist du so karg?

WELLGUNDE

So miserly, too?   So geizig beim Kauf?

FLOSSHILDE

When maidens   Freigebig
have asked a boon, men should give!   solltest Frauen du sein.

SIEGFRIED

But then if I waste my wealth,   [86]   Verzehrt' ich an euch mein Gut,
I'm sure that my wife will scold.   des zürnte mir wohl mein Weib.

FLOSSHILDE

Is she so stern?   Sie ist wohl schlimm?

WELLGUNDE

She strikes you then?   Sie schlägt dich wohl?

WOGLINDE

Has the hero felt her hand?   Ihre Hand fühlt schon der Held!

They burst out laughing immoderately.

110

Well, laugh then if you will!	Nun lacht nur lustig zu!
In grief you will be left:	In Harm lass ich euch doch:
you ask me for the ring —	denn giert ihr nach dem Ring,
I'll never give it to you.	euch Nickern geb ich ihn nie!

The Rhinemaidens have resumed their dance.

FLOSSHILDE

So fair!	[87] So schön!

WELLGUNDE

So strong!	So stark!

WOGLINDE

And made for love!	So gehrenswert!

ALL THREE

How sad that he is mean to us!	Wie schade, dass er geizig ist!

They laugh and dive down. [86b]

SIEGFRIED
(*coming down lower*)

Why should I let them	Was leid ich doch
laugh and jeer?	das karge Lob?
Shall I bear their scorn?	Lass ich so mich schmähn?
If they return	Kämen sie wieder
to the shore again,	zum Wasserrand,
the ring gladly I'll give them.	den Ring könnten sie haben.
Hey! Hey hey! You merry	[87] He! he, he, ihr muntren
water maidens!	Wasserminnen!
Come back! I'll give you the ring!	Kommt rasch! Ich schenk euch den Ring!

He has drawn the ring from his finger and holds it on high. The Rhinemaidens rise again to the surface. They appear grave and solemn.

FLOSSHILDE

Now hold the ring,	[3] Behalt ihn, Held,
and guard it well,	und wahr ihn wohl,
and learn the evil that lies —	[6] bis du das Unheil errätst —

WOGLINDE AND WELLGUNDE

— that lies within the ring.	Das in dem Ring du hegst.

ALL THREE

Then you will be glad	Froh fühlst du dich dann,
you're freed by us from the curse.	[7b] befrein wir dich von dem Fluch.

SIEGFRIED
(*quietly places the ring back on his finger.*)

Then tell me what you know.	[6] So singet, was ihr wisst.

THE RHINEMAIDENS

Siegfried! Siegfried! Siegfried!	[5x] Siegfried! Siegfried! Siegfried!
Evil lies in that ring.	Schlimmes wissen wir dir.

WELLGUNDE

And if you keep it,	[6] Zu deinem Unheil
then you are doomed.	wahrst du den Ring!

ALL THREE

From the Rhine's pure gold	[3] Aus des Rheines Gold
the ring was forged.	ist der Reif geglüht.

WELLGUNDE

And the Niblung who made it
and lost it again —

Der ihn listig geschmiedet
und schmählich verlor —

ALL THREE

— laid a curse on it;
and all who own [23]
the ring — they must die,
doomed by the curse.

Der verfluchte ihn,
in fernster Zeit
zu zeugen den Tod
dem, der ihn trüg'.

FLOSSHILDE

As you killed the dragon —

Wie den Wurm du fälltest —

WELLGUNDE AND FLOSSHILDE

— so you shall die.

— so fällst auch du —

ALL THREE

You die today:
unless you obey [5x]
and give the ring to our care. [4, 17]

Und heute noch;
so heissen wir's dir,
tauschest den Ring du uns nicht —

WELLGUNDE AND FLOSSHILDE

Our holy Rhine
can release you.

— im tiefen Rhein
ihn zu bergen.

ALL THREE

Our stream alone [1b]
purges the curse! [25]
[38]

Nur seine Flut
sühnet den Fluch!

SIEGFRIED

So scheming and cunning — [86]
say no more!
By your craft you couldn't catch me,
by your threats still less can you frighten me!

Ihr listigen Frauen,
lasst das sein!
Traut' ich kaum eurem Schmeicheln,
euer Drohen schreckt mich noch minder!

THE RHINEMAIDENS

Siegfried! Siegfried! [5x]
Give heed to our words.
Siegfried! Fly from the curse! [25]
By Norns at dead of night [6, 62]
it was woven
in the rope of fate's decrees!

Siegfried! Siegfried!
Wir weisen dich wahr.
Weiche, weiche dem Fluch!
Ihn flochten nächtlich
webende Nornen
in des Urgesetzes Seil!

SIEGFRIED

My sword has shattered a spear: [9a]
in the rope of fate's
eternal decrees,
what though the Norns [6, 62]
have woven a curse —
Notung can cut it asunder! [27b, 46]
Though Fafner once warned me [52]
to flee the curse,
yet he could not teach me to fear. [7b]

Mein Schwert zerschwang einen Speer:
des Urgesetzes
ewiges Seil,
flochten sie wilde
Flüche hinein,
Notung zerhaut es den Nornen!
Wohl warnte mich einst
vor dem Fluch ein Wurm,
doch das Fürchten lehrt' er mich nicht!

(He contemplates the ring.) [4]

The world's wealth [8]
I could win me by this ring:
for a glance of love [87]
I would exchange it;
if you had smiled the ring would be yours.
But you threatened my limbs and my life:
now though the ring
had no worth at all,
you'd still not get it from me.

Der Welt Erbe
gewänne mir ein Ring:
für der Minne Gunst
miss ich ihn gern;
ich geb ihn euch, gönnt ihr mir Lust.
Doch bedroht ihr mir Leben und Leib:
fasste er nicht
eines Fingers Wert,
den Reif entringt ihr mir nicht!

112

My limbs and my life! —	[5x]	Denn Leben und Leib,
See! So		seht: — so —
freely I'd fling away!		werf ich sie weit von mir!

He lifts a clod of earth from the ground, holds it above his head, and with the last words throws it behind him.

THE RHINEMAIDENS

Come, sisters!	[86b]	Kommt, Schwestern!
Flee from this madman!		Schwindet dem Toren!
He thinks he is wise,		So weise und stark
he thinks he is strong,		verwähnt sich der Held,
but he's stupid and blind as a child!		als gebunden und blind er doch ist.

(They swim, wildly excited, in wide circles close to the shore.) [87]

Vows he swore once —	Eide schwur er —
he's false to his vows!	und achtet sie nicht!
He was wise once —	Runen weiss er —
he's wise no more!	und rät sie nicht!

FLOSSHILDE, THEN WOGLINDE

A glorious gift	[65]	Ein hehrstes Gut
lay in his grasp.		ward ihm gegönnt.

ALL THREE

Now he has lost it,	Dass er's verworfen,
thrown it away.	weiss er nicht.

FLOSSHILDE

But the ring —	Nur den Ring —

WELLGUNDE

— that will bring his death, —	— der zum Tod ihm taugt —

ALL THREE

— the ring he will not surrender!	[6]	— den Reif nur will er sich wahren!
Farewell, Siegfried!		Leb wohl, Siegfried!
You die today;		Ein stolzes Weib
and your ring returns to Brünnhild;		wird noch heut dich Argen beerben,
by her, our prayer will be heard.		Sie beut uns bessres Gehör.
To her! To her! To her!		Zu ihr! Zu ihr! Zu ihr!

(They return quickly to their dance, in which they slowly swim away to the back. Siegfried looks after them, smiling, then places one foot on a rock on the shore and stays there with his chin resting on his hand.) [87, 86, 86b]

Weialala leia.	Weialala leia,
Wallala leialala.	Wallala leialala.

SIEGFRIED

On land and now on water	Im Wasser wie am Lande
I have learnt what women are:	lernt' nun ich Weiberart:
for if you defy their smiles,	wer nicht ihrem Schmeicheln traut,
they try with threats to scare you;	den schrecken sie mit Drohen;
and if you scorn their threats,	wer dem nun kühnlich trotzt,
they sting you with scolding words!	dem kommt dann ihr Keifen dran.

(The Rhinemaidens have now quite disappeared.)

And yet,	Und doch,
were I not Gutrun's husband,	trüg' ich nicht Gutrun' Treu'
I'd try to capture	der zieren Frauen eine
one of those pretty maids — make her mine!	hätt' ich mir frisch gezähmt!

He looks calmly after them.

THE RHINEMAIDENS
(very far away)

La, la!	La, la!

Hunting horns are heard approaching on the cliff top. [23, 73]

Scene Two.

Hoiho! Hoiho!

Siegfried starts from a dreamy reverie and answers the call with his horn. [45]

VASSALS
(off stage)

Hoiho! Hoiho! Hoiho! Hoiho!

SIEGFRIED
(answering)

Hoiho! Hoiho! Hoihe! Hoiho! Hoiho! Hoihe!

HAGEN
(appears on the cliff, followed by Gunther. Seeing Siegfried:) [45]

At last we have found you;	Finden wir endlich,
where have you been hiding?	wohin du flogest?

SIEGFRIED

Join me here! Here it's fresh and cool!　[87] Kommt herab! Hier ist's frisch und kühl!

The vassals all reach the top of the cliff and now come down with Hagen and Gunther. [45, 73, 87]

HAGEN

Let's rest a while,	Hier rasten wir
for here we can feast!	und rüsten das Mahl.

(They lay the game in a heap.)

Lay down the game here,	Lasst ruhn die Beute
and open the wine-skins!	und bietet die Schläuche!

(Wine-skins and drinkhorns are produced. All settle down.)

You drove the game away from us;　[68x, 72]	Der uns das Wild verscheuchte,
so let us hear the story	nun sollt ihr Wunder hören,
of Siegfried and his chase.	was Siegfried sich erjagt.

SIEGFRIED
(laughing)

I've nothing much to tell,	Schlimm steht es um mein Mahl:
instead I'll ask you:	von eurer Beute
Can I share your meal?	bitte ich für mich.

HAGEN

No game at all?　Du beutelos?

SIEGFRIED

I set forth after a bear,　[87, 45]	Auf Waldjagd zog ich aus,
but water-fowl were all that I found:	doch Wasserwild zeigte sich nur.
if I'd known that I'd have caught them,	War ich dazu recht beraten,
and I'd have bagged a brood	drei wilde Wasservögel
of frolicsome water maidens;	hätt' ich euch wohl gefangen,
they sang on the Rhine their warning:　[86]	die dort auf dem Rhein mir sangen,
my death awaits me today.　[5x]	erschlagen würd' ich noch heut.

He sits down between Gunther and Hagen. Gunther shudders and looks darkly at Hagen. [78]

HAGEN

A cruel and evil hunt,　[5x, 72]	Das wäre üble Jagd,
if the bear should get away,	wenn den Beutelosen selbst
and then a boar should kill you!	ein lauernd Wild erlegte!

SIEGFRIED

I'm thirsty!　[88]　Mich dürstet!

114

(while he has a drinking-horn filled for Siegfried, and then hands it to him)

I've heard it rumoured, Siegfried,	Ich hörte sagen, Siegfried,
that when the birds are singing	[53a]der Vögel Sangessprache
you know what they say:	verstündest du wohl.
but can that be true?	[53b] So wäre das wahr?

SIEGFRIED

For a long while I've paid	Seit lange acht ich
no heed to their song.	das Lallens nicht mehr.

(He grasps the horn and turns with it toward Gunther. He drinks, and then offers Gunther the horn.) [87, 73]

Drink, Gunther, drink!	Trink, Gunther, trink!
Your brother drinks with you!	Dein Bruder bringt es dir!

GUNTHER
(looks into the horn broodingly and gloomily; dully:) [66, 76e, 5x, 78]

The wine is thin and pale!	Du mischtest matt und bleich:

(more gloomily still)

Your blood alone I see!	dein Blut allein darin!

SIEGFRIED
(laughing)

I'll mingle it with your blood!	[76c]So misch es mit dem deinen!

(He pours from Gunther's horn into his own so that it overflows.) [73, 13a]

Now yours and mine run over;	Nun floss gemischt es über:
let earth, our mother,	der Mutter Erde
receive the noble draught.	lass das ein Labsal sein!

GUNTHER
(with a deep sigh)

You overjoyful man!	Du überfroher Held!

SIEGFRIED
(softly to Hagen)

He broods on Brünnhilde's words?	[18] Ihm macht Brünnhilde Müh?

HAGEN
(softly to Siegfried)

Her voice is not so clear	Verstünd' er sie so gut
as the song of birds to you!	[88] wie du der Vögel Sang!

SIEGFRIED

Since women have sung their songs to	Seit Frauen ich singen hörte,
me,	[87, 58d]
I've cared for the birdsong no more.	vergass ich der Vöglein ganz.

HAGEN

Yet once you knew it well?	[88] Doch einst vernahmst du sie?

SIEGFRIED
(turning with animation to Gunther)

Hi, Gunther,	[72] Hei, Gunther,
unhappy man!	grämlicher Mann!
If you would like,	[17] Dankst du es mir,
I'll sing you the story	so sing ich dir Mären
of all my young adventures.	aus meinen jungen Tagen.

GUNTHER

I'd like to hear.	Die hör ich gern.

All gather round Siegfried, who alone sits upright while the others lie stretched out. [53]

HAGEN

So sing to us!	So singe, Held!

Mime was
a hideous dwarf;
and he brought me up,
driven by greed,
so that when I'd grown
to be manly and strong,
I could kill for him a dragon
who long had guarded a hoard of gold.
He made me his pupil,
and taught me forging.
One task that Mime
could not achieve,
his pupil's skill
could teach to the master:
out of a shattered weapon's splinters,
new, I fashioned a sword.
My father's sword,
forged by his son,
sharp and strong,
glittering Notung.
Then I was judged
ready to fight;
so into the wood we went ...
Soon the dragon, Fafner, was dead.

Now you must hear
what happened next:
wondrous things I can tell you.
From the dragon's blood
my fingers were burning;
I raised them up to my mouth:
and when the blood
had but wetted my tongue,
then what the birds were singing —
I heard that song like speech.
In the tree above me one sang:
'Hi! Siegfried inherits
the Nibelung gold!
Oh, there it is waiting
within that cave!
There is the Tarnhelm, whose magic
will serve him for glorious deeds;
and if he discovers the ring,
it will make him the lord of the world!'

[17]   Mime hiess
ein mürrischer Zwerg:
in des Neides Zwang
zog er mich auf,
dass einst das Kind,
wann kühn es erwuchs,
einen Wurm ihm fällt' im Wald,
der faul dort hütet einen Hort.
Er lehrte mich schmieden
und Erze schmelzen;
doch was der Künstler
selber nicht konnt',
des Lehrlings Mute
musst' es gelingen:
eines zerschlagnen Stahles Stücken
[27] neu zu schweissen zum Schwert.
[27b]   Des Vater Wehr
fügt' ich mir neu:
nagelfest
schuf ich mir Notung.
Tüchtig zum Kampf
dünkt' er dem Zwerg;
[21] der führte mich nun zum Wald;
dort fällt' ich Fafner, den Wurm.

Jetzt aber merkt
wohl auf die Mär:
[31] Wunder muss ich euch melden.
Von des Wurmes Blut
mir brannten die Finger;
sie führt' ich kühlend zum Mund:
[88]   kaum netzt' ein wenig
die Zunge das Nass,
was da die Vöglein sangen,
das konnt' ich flugs verstehn.
Auf den Ästen sass es und sang:
[53c]   'Hei! Siegfried gehört nun
der Nibelungen Hort!
O fänd' in der Höhle
den Hort er jetzt!
[53d] Wollt' er den Tarnhelm gewinnen,
der taugt' ihm zu wonniger Tat!
Doch möcht' er den Ring sich erraten,
der macht' ihn zum Walter der Welt!'

Ring and Tarnhelm
then did you find?

Ring und Tarnhelm
trugst du nun fort?

The woodbird, what did it say then?   Das Vöglein hörtest du wieder?

Ring and Tarnhelm —
both I had found.
I heard again
the song of the woodbird;
it sat above me and sang:
'Hi! Siegfried discovered
the Tarnhelm and ring.
Now, let him beware
of the treacherous dwarf!
For Mime is planning to kill him
and take all the gold for himself:

[31]   Ring und Tarnhelm
hatt' ich gerafft:
da lauscht' ich wieder
dem wonnigen Laller;
der sass im Wipfel und sang:
[53c]   'Hei, Siegfried gehört nun
der Helm und der Ring.
O traute er Mime,
dem Treulosen, nicht!
[53d] Ihm sollt' er den Hort nur erheben;
nun lauert er listig am Weg:

See him lurking, waiting for Siegfried!	nach dem Leben trachtet er Siegfried.
Oh, Siegfried, beware of Mime!'	O traute Siegfried nicht Mime!'

HAGEN

The warning was true?	[31]	Es mahnte dich gut?

FOUR VASSALS

What happened to Mime?	Vergaltest du Mime?

SIEGFRIED

A poisonous drink	Mit tödlichem Tranke
he'd brewed for my death;	trat er zu mir;
scared and shaking,	bang und stotternd
he showed me his baseness:	gestand er mir Böses:
Notung ended his life!	Notung streckte den Strolch!

HAGEN
(laughing harshly)

Unable to forge it,	[17]	Was nicht er geschmiedet,
still he could feel it!		schmeckte doch Mime!

TWO VASSALS
(one after the other)

What heard you then from the woodbird?	[88]	Was wies das Vöglein dich wieder?

HAGEN
(has another drinking-horn filled and squeezes the juice of a herb into it.)

Drink first, hero,	[72]	Trink' erst, Held,
from my horn.		aus meinem Horn:
I have here a noble drink;		ich würzte dir holden Trank,
let its freshening power wake your		die Erinnerung hell dir zu wecken,
remembrance,		

(He hands Siegfried the horn.) [18]

so none of the past escapes you.	dass Fernes nicht dir entfalle!

SIEGFRIED
(looks thoughtfully into the horn, and then drinks slowly.) [71, 66, 31, 65]

In grief I watched		In Leid zu dem Wipfel
the branches above;		lauscht' ich hinauf;
the bird was there, and sang:		da sass es noch und sang:
'Hi! Siegfried is free	[53]	'Hei, Siegfried erschlug nun
from the evil dwarf!		den schlimmen Zwerg!
Next he must awake		Jetzt wüsst' ich ihm noch
his glorious bride:		das herrlichste Weib.
high on a mountain she sleeps,		Auf hohem Felsen sie schläft,
guarded by threatening flames.		Feuer umbrennt ihren Saal;
Who goes through the fire,	[4]	durchschritt' er die Brunst,
wakens the bride,		weckt' er die Braut,
Brünnhilde then shall be his!'		Brünnhilde wäre dann sein!'

HAGEN

And did you take	Und folgtest du
the woodbird's counsel?	des Vögleins Rate?

SIEGFRIED

Yes, I arose	Rasch ohne Zögern
and went on my way,	zog ich nun aus,

(Gunther listens with increasing astonishment.)

till I came to that fiery peak.	[14]	bis den feurigen Fels ich traf:
I passed through those dangers;		die Lohe durchschritt ich
I found the maid ...		und fand zum Lohn
sleeping ... my glorious bride!	[11a, 43]	schlafend — ein wonniges Weib
In shining armour she lay.		in lichter Waffen Gewand.
The helmet		Den Helm löst' ich
I took from her head;		der herrlichen Maid;

117

my kiss awakened the bride.
Oh, then like burning fire
I was held by lovely Brünnhilde's arms!

mein Kuss erweckte sie kühn:
[56] oh, wie mich brünstig da umschlang
der schönen Brünnhilde Arm!

GUNTHER
(*springing up with the utmost dismay*)

What hear I!

Was hör ich?

Two ravens fly up out of a bush, circle over Siegfried, and then fly away towards the Rhine.

HAGEN

And can you tell
what those ravens have said?

Errätst du auch
dieser Raben Geraun'?

(*Siegfried stands up suddenly and, turning his back to Hagen, looks after the ravens.*) [23, 5x]
Vengeance! That's what they cry!   Rache rieten sie mir!

Hagen thrusts his spear into Siegfried's back. Gunther — too late — seizes his arm. Siegfried swings his shield up with both hands, as if to crush Hagen with it; his strength fails him; the shield falls backwards and he himself falls down on the shield. [39]

FOUR VASSALS
(*who have in vain tried to hold Hagen back:*)

Hagen, you've killed him!   [89] Hagen, was tust du?

TWO OTHERS

You murdered him!   Was tatest du?

GUNTHER

Hagen, you murdered him!   [38, 76e] Hagen, was tatest du?

HAGEN
(*gesturing at the outstretched body*)

Falsehood is punished.   Meineid rächt' ich!

He turns calmly away and goes alone, over the cliff top, where he is seen walking slowly through the dusk which began to fall when the ravens appeared. Gunther bends down, grief-stricken, over Siegfried. The vassals, filled with sympathy, surround the dying man.

SIEGFRIED

(*supported in a sitting position by two vassals, opens his eyes which are filled with radiance.*)

Brünnhilde!
Holiest bride!
Now wake! Wake from your slumber!
Who has forced you
back to your sleep?
Who bound you in slumber again?
Your bridegroom came,
to kiss you awake;
he frees you, again,
breaking your fetters.
He lives in Brünnhilde's love!
Ah! See those eyes,
open forever!
Ah! Feel her breathing,
loving and tender!
Joyful surrender!
Sweet are these terrors!
Brünnhild waits for me here!

[57] Brünnhilde,
heilige Braut,
Wach auf! Öffne dein Auge!
[38] Wer verschloss dich
wieder in Schlaf?
Wer band dich in Schlummer so bang?
Der Wecker kam;
[39] er küsst dich wach,
und aber der Braut
bricht er die Bande:
da lacht ihm Brünnhildes Lust!
[59] Ach, dieses Auge,
ewig nun offen!
Ach, dieses Atems
wonniges Wehen!
[58] Süsses Vergehen,
seliges Grauen —
[38] Brünnhild bietet mir — Gruss!

He sinks back and dies. The rest stand around him in sorrow without moving. Night has fallen. At Gunther's mute command the vassals raise Siegfried's body and carry it away in a solemn procession over the cliff top. Gunther follows beside the body. The moon breaks through the clouds, and lights up the funeral procession ever more brightly as it reaches the summit of the cliff. Then mists rise from the Rhine and gradually come forward to fill the whole stage, on which the funeral procession becomes invisible. During the musical interlude, the stage is completely veiled. When the mists divide again, the hall of the Gibichungs, as in the first act, is gradually revealed. [89, 31, 33, 29, 30, 27, 89b, 39, 64, 65]

118

Scene Three. *The Gibichung Hall. It is night. Moonlight is reflected on the Rhine.* [5x, 5b, 23, 64] *Gutrune comes from her room into the hall.* [75, 45]

GUTRUNE

Was that his horn?		War das sein Horn?
(She listens.) [5b]		
No!		Nein! Noch
He has not returned.		kehrt er nicht heim.
Dreams of evil		Schlimme Träume
drove away my sleep.	[45]	störten mir den Schlaf!
Wild neighs I heard from his horse;	[34]	Wild wieherte sein Ross;
Brünnhilde's laughter		Lachen Brünnhildes
then woke me from sleep.		weckte mich auf.
And was it she	[5x, 5b, 4, 65]	Wer war das Weib,
I saw there, walking by the shore?		das ich zum Ufer schreiten sah?
I fear this Brünnhild!		Ich fürchte Brünnhilde!
Is she still here?	[38]	Ist sie daheim?

(She listens at the door on the right, and calls softly.)

Brünnhild! Brünnhild!		Brünnhild! Brünnhild!
Are you there?		Bist du wach?

(She opens the door hesitantly, and looks into the room.) [65]

No, she has gone.		Leer das Gemach.
Then it was she		So war es sie,
whom I saw walking there.	[5b]	die ich zum Rheine schreiten sah!

(She shudders, and listens to some distant sound.) [73]

Was that his horn?		War das sein Horn?
No!		Nein!
All silent!		Öd alles!
Ah, if Siegfried were back!	[73, 78]	Säh' ich Siegfried nur bald!

She sets out to return to her room, but hearing Hagen's voice, she stops and, stricken with fear, remains motionless for a while.

HAGEN
(calling from without, as he approaches)

Hoiho! Hoiho!	[5x, 78]	Hoiho! Hoiho!
Awake! Awake!		Wacht auf! Wacht auf!
Torches, torches!		Lichte! Lichte!
Light the torches!		Helle Brände!
Hunters come back		Jagdbeute
with their prey.		bringen wir heim.
Hoiho! Hoiho!		Hoiho! Hoiho!

(The torch light outside increases. Hagen enters the hall.) [73]

Up, Gutrun!		Auf, Gutrun!
and greet your Siegfried!		Begrüsse Siegfried!
That mighty man	[64]	Der starke Held,
is coming home.		er kehret heim!

GUTRUNE
(in great terror)

What is this? Hagen!	[78]	Was geschah, Hagen?
I heard not his horn!	[45]	Nicht hört' ich sein Horn!

Men and women, with torches and firebrands, accompany the procession returning home with Siegfried's body; Gunther is among them.

HAGEN

That mighty man	[76e]	Der bleiche Held,
will sound it no more;		nicht bläst er es mehr;
no more will he hunt,		nicht stürmt er zur Jagd,
no more will he fight,		zum Streite nicht mehr,
no more will he woo lovely women.	[7b]	noch wirbt er um wonnige Frauen.

GUTRUNE
(with increasing horror)

Who is coming there?   [45] Was bringen die?

The procession reaches the middle of the hall and the vassals set down the body on a mound.
[39]

HAGEN

A ferocious boar has slain him;   [5x] Eines wilden Ebers Beute:
Siegfried, your husband, is dead.   Siegfried, deinen toten Mann.

Gutrune cries out and falls on the body. General horror and mourning.

GUNTHER
(supporting his swooning sister)

Gutrun! Gentle sister!   Gutrun, holde Schwester,
  Hear me and answer;   hebe dein Auge,
  speak to me!   schweige mir nicht!

GUTRUNE
(coming to herself again)

Siegfried! Siegfried is murdered!   [89] Siegfried — Siegfried erschlagen!
(She repels Gunther violently.)

No! Treacherous brother!   Fort, treuloser Bruder,
You murderer of my husband!   du Mörder meines Mannes!
  Oh help me! Help me!   O Hülfe, Hülfe!
  Sorrow! Sorrow!   Wehe! Wehe!
My husband Siegfried is murdered!   Sie haben Siegfried erschlagen!

GUNTHER

Cast not the blame on me,   Nicht klage wider mich!
but cast the blame on Hagen.   Dort klage wider Hagen;
He is the boar who killed him;   [45] er ist der verfluchte Eber,
by Hagen's spear he was slain.   der diesen Edlen zerfleischt'.

HAGEN

And you blame me for that?   Bist du mir gram darum?

GUNTHER

Yes, I blame you;   [82] Angst und Unheil
  curse you forever!   greife dich immer!

HAGEN
(stepping forward with terrible defiance)

Well then! I own that I killed him: [85] Ja denn! Ich hab ihn erschlagen.
  I, Hagen,   Ich, Hagen,
  sent him to death.   schlug ihn zu Tod.
With my spear I took his life,   [76e]Meinem Speer war er gespart,
for by that spear he swore.   bei dem er Meineid sprach.
Rightly he fell to me;   Heiliges Beuterecht
now I shall be rewarded: hab ich mir nun errungen:
and so I claim here the ring.   [6] d'rum fordr' ich hier diesen Ring.

GUNTHER

Stand back! For I declare   Zurück! Was mir verfiel,
that golden ring is mine!   sollst nimmer du empfahn.

HAGEN

You vassals, grant me my right.   Ihr Mannen, richtet mein Recht!

GUNTHER

That ring is Gutrune's treasure,   Rührst du an Gutrunes Erbe,
misbegotten Niblung son!   schamloser Albensohn?

HAGEN
(*drawing his sword*)

The Niblung's treasure   [23]   Des Alben Erbe
comes to me, his son.   fordert so sein Sohn!

(*He rushes upon Gunther, who defends himself; they fight. Vassals throw themselves between them. Hagen strikes Gunther dead.*) [6, 5x, 5b]

Mine, the ring!   Her den Ring!

He reaches towards Siegfried's hand, which raises itself threateningly. Gutrune and the women cry out in fear. All remain motionless with terror. Brünnhilde begins to walk forward from the back, firmly and solemnly. [27, 25]

BRÜNNHILDE
(*still in the background*) .

Peace with your cries   [24, 25]   Schweigt eures Jammers
of useless lament!   jauchzenden Schwall.
For you all have betrayed me;   Das ihr alle verrietet,
for vengeance here I have come.   [38]   zur Rache schreitet sein Weib.
(*She comes further forward.*)
Children here   Kinder hört' ich
are whining for their mother   greinen nach der Mutter,
because some milk has been spilled;   da süsse Milch sie verschüttet:
I hear no cries   doch nicht erklang mir
of true lamentation   würdige Klage,
to mourn this hero's worth.   [37]   des höchsten Helden wert.

GUTRUNE
(*getting up impetuously*)

Brünnhilde! Cruel and envious!   Brünnhilde! Neiderboste!
You brought this shame on our house;   Du brachtest uns diese Not:
your words aroused the men against him.   die du die Männer ihm verhetztest,
Cursed be the day you came!   weh, dass du dem Haus genaht!

BRÜNNHILDE

Poor creature, peace!   Armselige, schweig!
For you and he were not wed;   [73]   Sein Eheweib warst du nie,
his mistress,   als Buhlerin
but never his wife!   bandest du ihn.
But I was his own true wife;   [56]   Sein Mannesgemahl bin ich,
eternal devotion he'd sworn,   der ewige Eide er schwur,
and Siegfried and Brünnhild were one!   eh Siegfried je dich ersah.

GUTRUNE
(*breaking out in sudden despair*)

Accursed Hagen!   [71]   Verfluchter Hagen,
By your advice I gave him   dass du das Gift mir rietest,
the drink that made him forget!   das ihr den Gatten entrückt!
Ah, sorrow!   Ach, Jammer!
My eyes are opened.   Wie jäh nun weiss ich's,
Brünnhild was his true love,   [75]   Brünnhild war die Traute,
whom through the drink he forgot!   die durch den Trank er vergass!

Filled with shame, she turns away from Siegfried and, abandoning herself to grief, bends over Gunther's body; so she remains, motionless, till the end. Hagen, defiantly leaning on his spear, stands sunk in gloomy brooding, on the opposite side. [38]

BRÜNNHILDE
(*alone in the centre; after remaining long absorbed in contemplation of Siegfried's face, first with profound shock, then with almost overwhelming despair, she turns to the men and women in solemn exaltation. To the vassals:*)

Sturdy branches,   [60]   Starke Scheite
building his pyre   schichtet mir dort
now bring to the shore of the Rhine!   am Rande des Rheins zuhauf!
Bright and clear,   Hoch und hell
kindle the flame: [14]   lodre die Glut,

121

let the hero blaze	[39] die den edlen Leib
in splendour and radiance on high.	[25] des hehrsten Helden verzehrt.
His horse bring to my side;	[34] Sein Ross führet daher,
he and I together must join him.	dass mit mir dem Recken es folge;
I shall share that pure, holy flame	denn des Helden heiligste
with the hero;	Ehre zu teilen,
we both shall blaze in the fire.	verlangt mein eigener Leib.
Obey Brünnhild's command!	Vollbringt Brünnhildes Wort!

(During the following, the younger men raise a huge funeral pyre of logs before the hall, near the bank of the Rhine: women decorate this with coverings on which they strew plants and flowers. Brünnhilde becomes again absorbed in contemplation of Siegfried's body. Her features become increasingly transfigured with tenderness.) [59]

The sun in splendour	Wie Sonne lauter
shines from his eyes:	strahlt mir sein Licht:
the purest hero,	der Reinste war er,
though he was false!	[90] der mich verriet!
Untrue to Brünnhild,	Die Gattin trügend,
true to friendship!	treu dem Freunde,
From the wife who loved him,	vor der eignen Trauten,
while he betrayed her,	einzig ihm teuer,
he was barred by his sword.	[27] schied er sich durch sein Schwert.
Never was man	Echter als er
more loyal to friendship;	[90] schwur keiner Eide;
never was man	treuer als er
more true to his promise;	hielt keiner Verträge;
never was known	lautrer als er
love more faithful.	liebte kein andrer.
And yet he was faithless,	Und doch, alle Eide,
broke every promise;	alle Verträge,
the truest of lovers —	die treueste Liebe
none falser than he!	[79] trog keiner wie er!

Know you why that was?	[37] Wisst ihr, wie das ward?
	(looking upward)
Look down, you guardians,	[8] O ihr, der Eide
look down and hear me!	Heilige Hüter!
Turn your regard	Lenkt euren Blick
on my shame and my grief;	auf mein blühendes Leid,
and learn your eternal disgrace!	[37] erschaut eure ewige Schuld!
And Wotan, hear,	[41] Meine Klage hör,
you mighty god!	du hehrster Gott!
By his most valiant deed	Durch seine tapferste Tat,
he fulfilled your desire,	dir so tauglich erwünscht,
but he was forced	weihtest du den,
to share in your curse —	der sie gewirkt,
that curse which has doomed your downfall.	dem Fluche, dem du verfielest.
He, truest of all men,	Mich musste
betrayed me,	der reinste verraten,
that I in grief might grow wise!	[38] dass wissend würde ein Weib!

Now I know what must be.	Weiss ich nun, was dir frommt?
All things, all things,	Alles, alles,
all I know now;	[5x] alles weiss ich,
all to me is revealed!	alles ward mir nun frei!
Call back your ravens	Auch deine Raben
hovering round me;	hör ich rauschen;
they'll bring to you those tidings	mit bang ersehnter Botschaft
you have both feared and desired.	[23] send ich die beiden nun heim.
Rest now, rest now, O God!	[8d, 60, 8e] Ruhe, ruhe, du Gott!

(She gives a sign to the vassals to place Siegfried's body on the pyre; at the same time she draws the ring from Siegfried's finger and gazes at it thoughtfully.) [60, 25, 1b]

My heritage	Mein Erbe nun
I claim from the hero.	[6] nehm ich zu eigen.

Accursed gold!		Verfluchter Reif!
Terrible ring!		Furchtbarer Ring!
My hand grasps you		Dein Gold fass ich
to cast you away.`		und geb es nun fort.
You sisters	[4, 87]	Der Wassertiefe
who are wise and graceful,		weise Schwestern,
you Rhinemaids who dwell in the waters,	[2]	des Rheines schwimmende Töchter,
I shall obey your advice.		euch dank ich redlichen Rat.
What you desire		Was ihr begehrt,
I'll give to you:		ich geb es euch:
and from my ashes	[3]	aus meiner Asche
gather your treasure!		nehmt es zu eigen!
This fire, burning my frame,		Das Feuer, das mich verbrennt,
cleanses the curse from the ring!		rein'ge vom Fluche den Ring!
There in the Rhine,	[86]	Ihr in der Flut
the ring shall be pure;		löset ihn auf,
preserve it,	[4]	und lauter bewahrt
and guard your shining gold	[6]	das lichte Gold,
whose theft has caused all our woe.	[23]	das euch zum Unheil geraubt.

(She has placed the ring on her finger, and now turns to the pile of logs on which Siegfried's body is laid. She seizes a great fire-brand from one of the vassals and gestures towards the back.) [9a]

Fly home, you ravens!	[13b, 14]	Fliegt heim, ihr Raben!
Tell your lord the tidings		Raunt es eurem Herrn,
that here by the Rhine you have learned!		was hier am Rhein ihr gehört!
Past Brünnhilde's mountain	[13a]	An Brünnhildes Felsen
take your flight,		fahrt vorbei.
where Loge is burning!		Der dort noch lodert,
Summon Loge to Walhall!		weiset Loge nach Walhall!
For the gods' destruction	[25, 24]	Denn der Götter Ende
soon shall be here.		dämmert nun auf.
I cast now the flame	[5x]	So — werf ich den Brand
at Walhall's glorious height.		in Walhalls prangende Burg.

* [You, flourishing mankind's	* Ihr, blühenden Lebens
remaining race,	bleibend Geschlecht: ·
listen now to what I	was ich nun euch melde,
have to tell you:	merket es wohl! —
You'll see by the kindling fire	Saht ihr vom zündenden Brand
Siegfried and Brünnhilde consumed;	Siegfried und Brünnhild' verzehrt;
you'll see the Rhinemaidens	saht ihr des Rheines Töchter
returning the ring to the deep;	zur Tiefe entführen den Ring:
to the North then	nach Norden dann
look through the night.	blickt durch die Nacht!
There, shining in the sky,	Erglänzt dort am Himmel
glows a sacred fire;	ein heiliges Glüh'n,
so understand	so wisset all' —
that you're watching Valhalla's end.	dass ihr Walhall's Ende gewahrt! —

Vanished like air	Verging wie Hauch
is the race of gods;	der Götter Geschlecht,
without rulership	lass' ohne Walter
I leave the world behind;	die Welt ich zurück:
my wisdom's holiest hoard	meines heiligsten Wissens Hort
I assign to the world.	weis' ich der Welt nun zu. —
Not goods nor gold	Nicht Gut, nicht Gold,
for godly state;	noch göttliche Pracht;
not house nor hearth	nicht Haus, nicht Hof,
for lordly pomp;	noch herrischer Prunk:
not empty treaties'	nicht trüber Verträge

---

* The following lines, here translated by Elizabeth Forbes, were not set to music: 'As these verses, because their meaning was already conveyed with the greatest clarity by the musical effects of the drama, became unnecessary in live performance, they were not set by the composer —' Richard Wagner

treacherous bonds		trügender Bund,
for false tradition's		noch heuchelnder Sitte
pitiless law:		hartes Gesetz:
blessed in joy and sorrow,		selig in Lust und Leid
only love I bequeath!]		lässt — die Liebe nur sein! —

(She flings the brand on the pyre, which quickly breaks out into bright flames. Two ravens fly up from the rocks on the shore and disappear in the background. [8a, 13a] Brünnhilde sees her horse which has been led in by two young men. She hastens towards it, takes hold of it and quickly removes the bridle; then she leans over it confidingly.) [34, 35]

Grane, my horse!		Grane, mein Ross,
I greet my friend!		sei mir gegrüsst!
Can you tell, my friend,		Weisst du auch, mein Freund,
to where I must lead you?		wohin ich dich führe?
In fiery glory	[40]	Im Feuer leuchtend,
blazes your lord,	[39]	liegt dort dein Herr,
Siegfried, my hero and love.		Siegfried, mein seliger Held.
To follow your master,	[34, 35]	Dem Freunde zu folgen,
Oh! Are you neighing?		wieherst du freudig?
Lured by the fire,	[14]	Lockt dich zu ihm
the light and its laughter?		die lachende Lohe?
I too am yearning	[40]	Fühl! meine Brust auch,
to join him there;		wie sie entbrennt;
glorious radiance		helles Feuer
has seized on my heart.		das Herz mir erfasst,
I shall embrace him,		ihn zu umschlingen,
united with him,		unschlossen von ihm,
in sacred yearning,		in mächtigster Minne
with him ever one!		vermählt ihm zu sein!
Hiayoho! Grane!	[39, 40]	Heiajoho! Grane!
Ride to your master!		Grüss deinen Herren!
Siegfried! Siegfried! See!		Siegfried! Siegfried! Sieh!
Brünnhild greets you as wife!		Selig grüsst dich dein Weib!

She has mounted the horse, and leaps with a single bound into the blazing pyre. [34, 35] The flames immediately blaze up so that they fill the whole space in front of the hall, and appear to seize on the building itself. The men and women press to the extreme front in terror. When the whole space of the stage seems filled with fire, the glow suddenly subsides, and only a cloud of smoke remains; this drifts to the background and lies there on the horizon as a dark bank of cloud. At the same time the Rhine overflows its banks in a mighty flood which pours over the fire. On the waves the three Rhinemaidens swim forwards and now appear above the pyre. Hagen, who since the incident of the ring has observed Brünnhilde's behaviour with increasing anxiety, is seized with great alarm at the appearance of the Rhinemaidens. He hastily throws aside spear, shield, and helmet and rushes like a madman into the flood. [14, 42, 5x, 4]

HAGEN

Give back the ring!	[23]	Zurück vom Ring!

Woglinde and Wellgunde twine their arms around his neck and draw him with them into the depths as they swim away. [86b] Flosshilde, swimming in front of the others towards the back, joyously holds up on high the regained ring. [2, 1c] Through the cloudbank, which has settled on the horizon, a red glow breaks out with increasing brightness. By its light, the three Rhinemaidens are seen, swimming in circles, merrily playing with the ring on the calmer waters of the Rhine, which has gradually returned to its bed. [8, 40] From the ruins of the fallen hall, the men and women, in great agitation, watch the growing fire-light in the heavens. When this reaches its greatest brightness, the hall of Walhall is seen, in which gods and heroes sit assembled, just as Waltraute described them in the first act. [8, 60] Bright flames seize on the hall of the gods. [39, 25] When the gods are entirely hidden by the flames, the curtain falls. [40]

Selective discography *by Cathy Peterson*

	W. Furtwängler	*W. Furtwängler*	*G. Solti*	*K. Böhm*
Conductor				
Orchestra/ Opera House	**La Scala**	**Rome Radio**	**Vienna State Opera**	**Bayreuth Festival**
Date	*1950*	*1953*	*1964*	*1967*
Brünnhilde	K. Flagstad	M. Mödl	B. Nilsson	B. Nilsson
Siegfried	M. Lorenz	L. Suthaus	W. Windgassen	W. Windgassen
Gunther	J. Hermann	A. Poell	D. Fischer-Dieskau	T. Stewart
Alberich	A. Pernerstorfer	A. Pernerstorfer	G. Neidlinger	G. Neidlinger
Hagen	L. Weber	J. Greindl	G. Frick	J. Greindl
Gutrune	H. Konetzni	S. Jurinac	C. Watson	L. Dvöraková
UK disc number	CFE 101 (part of complete *Ring*)	RLS 702 (part of complete *Ring*)	414 115-1	6747 037 (part of complete *Ring*)
UK tape number	–	–	414 115-4	–
US disc number	–	–	414 115-1	–
US tape number	–	–	414 115-4	–

Conductor Orchestra/ Opera House Date	H. von Karajan Berlin PO 1969/70	R. Goodall English National Opera 1977	P. Boulez Bayreuth Festival 1979/80	M. Janowski Dresden Staatskapelle 1983
Brünnhilde	H. Dernesch	R. Hunter	G. Jones	J. Altmeyer
Siegfried	H. Brilioth	A. Remedios	M. Jung	R. Kollo
Gunther	T. Stewart	N. Welsby	F. Mazura	H. Nocker
Alberich	Z. Kélémen	D. Hammond-Stroud	H. Becht	S. Nimsgern
Hagen	K. Ridderbusch	A. Haugland	F. Hubner	M. Salminen
Gutrune	G. Janowitz	M. Curphey	J. Altmeyer	N. Sharp
UK disc number	2740 148	SLS 5118	6769 073	301 817
UK tape number	3378 048	TC SLS 5118	—	501 817
US disc number	2721 006	—	6769 073	301 817
US tape number	3378 048	—	—	501 817

Highlights

Conductor	*C. Mackerras*
Conductor/Opera House	**London Philharmonic**
Date	*1972*
Brünnhilde	R. Hunter
Siegfried	A. Remedios

UK disc number	CFP 4403
UK tape number	TC CFP 4403

The Solti *Götterdämmerung* remains the classic modern version for the first time listener. The ENO version, recorded live at the London Coliseum, vividly captures the impact of Goodall's Wagner performances during the 1970s. Finally, for those interested in hearing the outstanding Brünnhilde of the 20th century under the inspired conducting of Fürtwängler, the live La Scala *Götterdämmerung* is essential listening.

For a detailed analysis of the history of *Götterdämmerung* on records, the reader is referred to Alan Blyth's article on *The Ring* in *Opera on Record* (Hutchinson, 1979).

Bibliography

Wagner wrote *Eine Mitteilung an meine Freunde* (*A Communication to my Friends*, 1851) as an introduction for them to the form of *The Ring* and *Oper und Drama* (*Opera and Drama*, 1852) sets out these new theories of opera. Both essays are included in *The Complete Prose Works of Richard Wagner*, translated by W. Ashton Ellis, which, although neither accurate nor fluent, is the most widely available translation (London, 1892-99; reprinted 1972). New translations of these and other important essays are to be published shortly by Cambridge. Robert Hartford's chronicle of *Bayreuth: The Early Years . . . as seen by the celebrated visitors and participants* (London, 1980), and the eye-witness account of the stage rehearsals for the first Bayreuth Festival in *Wagner Rehearsing the 'Ring'* by Heinrich Porges (trans. R. Jacobs, Cambridge, 1983) give a picture of the first cycles. The two massive volumes of *Cosima Wagner's Diaries* (I, 1869-77; II, 1873-83) make astonishing reading because of their frankness and comprehensiveness (ed. Gregor-Dellin and Mack, trans. G. Skelton, London, 1978, 1980). A new translation of Wagner's biography *My Life*, by A. Gray, ed. M. Whittall, has been published by Cambridge (1983).

Among the numerous biographical and musicological accounts of Wagner, there are two outstanding introductions: the Master Musicians volume by Barry Millington (London, 1984) and the New Grove volume by John Deathridge and Carl Dahlhaus (London, 1984). There are now a number of relatively modern studies in English devoted to *The Ring. Wagner's 'Ring': An Introduction* by Alan Blyth (London, 1980) contains simple musical synopses for the cycle in one compact volume. *I Saw the World End* by Deryck Cooke (Oxford, 1979) and *Wagner's 'Ring' and its Symbols* by Robert Donington (London, 1963) are brilliant and much more densely argued commentaries which have prompted in turn much discussion. Carl Dahlhaus's perceptive *Musicdramas of Richard Wagner* (trans. M. Whittall, Cambridge, 1980) includes chapters on the cycle.

In Christopher Wintle's article, aspects of the discussion of Old and New Testament parallels were suggested by a recent study of the Bible as fictional narrative by Dan Jacobson: *The Story of the Stories*, (Secker and Warburg, London, 1982). Ludwig Feuerbach's *The Essence of Christianity* is available in an English translation by George Eliot, (reprinted by Harper and Row, New York and London, 1957). Also of interest is a recent study of a production of *The Ring* at Bayreuth: Jean-Jacques Nattiez's *Tétralogies: Wagner, Boulez, Chéreau*, (Christian Bourgois, Paris, 1983). Theodor Adorno's *In Search of Wagner*, trans. Rodney Livingstone, is published by New Left Books, (London, 1981).

The Perfect Wagnerite by Bernard Shaw (London, 1898; New York, 1967) and *Wagner Nights* (London, 1949) by Ernest Newman are classic introductions to the cycle. The commentary of Paul Bekker in *Richard Wagner, His Life and Work* (trans. M. Bozman, New York, 1931, 1971) is still exceptionally rewarding. John Culshaw's account of recording the Decca *Ring* cycle is of interest to lovers of the score as well as record enthusiasts: *Ring Resounding* (London, 1967). *'The Ring': Anatomy of an Opera* by Stephen Fay and Roger Wood (London, 1984) is an exciting account of the preparation for the 1983 Bayreuth *Ring* cycle. For those interested in the staging of *The Ring*, Oswald Georg Bauer's study *Richard Wagner, The Stage Designs and Productions from the Premières to the Present* (Rizzoli, 1982) contains both accurate text and beautiful illustrations.

Contributors

Michael Tanner lectures in philosophy at Cambridge University. He contributed to *The Wagner Companion* (ed. Peter Burbidge and Richard Sutton), and writes articles on philosophy, criticism and opera.

Robin Holloway was born in 1943 and is a composer and music critic.

Christopher Wintle is Senior Lecturer in Music at Goldsmiths' College, University of London, and a member of the Editorial Board of *Music Analysis*.